TAKING DOWN THE CARTELS: EXAMINING UNITED STATES-MEXICO COOPERATION

HEARING

BEFORE THE

COMMITTEE ON HOMELAND SECURITY
HOUSE OF REPRESENTATIVES

ONE HUNDRED THIRTEENTH CONGRESS

SECOND SESSION

APRIL 2, 2014

Serial No. 113–60

Printed for the use of the Committee on Homeland Security

Available via the World Wide Web: http://www.gpo.gov/fdsys/

U.S. GOVERNMENT PRINTING OFFICE

88–779 PDF   WASHINGTON : 2014

For sale by the Superintendent of Documents, U.S. Government Printing Office
Internet: bookstore.gpo.gov   Phone: toll free (866) 512–1800; DC area (202) 512–1800
Fax: (202) 512–2250   Mail: Stop SSOP, Washington, DC 20402–0001

(II)

CONTENTS

TAKING DOWN THE CARTELS: EXAMINING UNITED STATES-MEXICO COOPERATION

Wednesday, April 2, 2014

U.S. HOUSE OF REPRESENTATIVES,
COMMITTEE ON HOMELAND SECURITY,
Washington, DC.

The committee met, pursuant to call, at 10:12 a.m., in Room 311, Cannon House Office Building, Hon. Michael T. McCaul [Chairman of the committee] presiding.

Present: Representatives McCaul, Broun, Duncan, Palazzo, Barletta, Brooks, Perry, Thompson, Sanchez, Jackson Lee, Clarke, Richmond, Barber, Payne, O'Rourke, and Vela.

Chairman McCAUL. Committee on Homeland Security will come to order. Committee is meeting today to examine the Federal Government's cooperative efforts with the government of Mexico to combat the drug cartels.

Mr. Broun—Dr. Broun, if you would, thank you.

I recognize myself for an opening statement.

Just last month Peña Nieto—his administration, in coordination with the U.S. law enforcement, took down the biggest drug kingpin in the world, El Chapo Guzmán, who was responsible for thousands of deaths and for violence that stretches across the globe. Leading up to Guzmán's capture, Mexican authorities also arrested a series of his significant lieutenants.

This past July President Peña Nieto's administration also captured Miguel Angel Trevino Morales, the leader of the Los Zetas cartel. This was the most significant arrest prior to Guzmán's and is indicative of President Peña Nieto's commitment to bring down the cartels.

Now we have an opportunity to examine the bilateral cooperation between our two nations that resulted in this progress and how we can build upon these successes to further combat the cartels.

I applaud Immigration and Customs Enforcement for their participation, along with DEA, U.S. Marshals, State Department, and Mexican authorities for this capture. The involvement of our agencies stems from the fact that Guzmán's reach went far beyond Mexican borders. He is Public Enemy No. 1 in Chicago and carries indictments in California, New York, and my home State of Texas.

As we all know, the capture of this drug lord was significant both symbolically and operationally to the Sinaloa Cartel. However, we know that drug trafficking organizations like this one will continue, and nowhere is it near extinction.

The best way for us to counter them is by working together, and today we are here to examine U.S.-Mexico cooperation in battling the cartels and the cartels' efforts on our homeland security.

Americans understand that the threat posed by drug traffickers is particularly intense along our Southwest Border. These organizations compete against each other for smuggling routes into the United States, creating a war zone that engulfs innocent people living in the region. The spillover violence in the United States stems from a variety of criminal activities which bring people and illicit goods into this country.

Drug trafficking organizations are highly agile. With billions of dollars in capital, these cartels are capable of corrupting officials and responding violently when targeted by law enforcement.

Additionally, these organizations are not constrained by boundaries, so often their crimes pass through many jurisdictions, creating an often challenging lanscape for law enforcement and reinforcing the need to work together to counter these criminals.

Cartels like the Sinaloas and the Zetas in Northern Mexico are growing their capabilities and infrastructure, and in doing so can facilitate the illicit flow of people, drugs, and weapons across our borders. There is a constant risk of these organizations partnering with foreign terrorist organizations, and the past arrest of an Iranian national suspected of plotting to assassinate the Saudi ambassador in the United States allegedly involved Mexican cartel members. This depth and coordination of criminal activity highlights the need for heightened awareness of the narcoterrorist nexus within the Mexican cartels.

Because of the threats to both the United States and Mexico stemming from organized crime, both of our nations share security objectives for our borders: Keep threats out but ensure the expeditious flow of commerce. Our respective law enforcement agencies have been working closely together to come to a common understanding of how to synchronize enforcement operations on each side of the border.

However, we cannot just focus on our shared border. Mexico must stop criminals long before they reach us.

As Mexico's economy improves, it is now seeing an increase in immigration from Central and South America. This will place a great burden on Mexico to better secure its southern border, and we are working, through the Mérida Initiative, to assist in not only technology applications but operational planning and training to support President Peña Nieto's goals as well as those of the United States.

As we saw last month, the ability to share information between the U.S. and Mexico's law enforcement agencies, as well as plan and conduct bilateral operations, is critical to achieving our mutual goal of combating the cartels.

As part of that effort, I and other Members of this committee recently sent a letter to Attorney General Holder and Secretary of State Kerry encouraging them to request Guzmán's extradition to the United States pursuant to the extradition treaty between our two nations. As with several other extraditions of narcotic traffickers from Mexico to the United States in recent years, this cooperation ensures these criminals will never threaten the law-abiding citizens of our two great nations ever again.

With the support of President Peña Nieto, we have the opportunity to work together to continue to strengthen our partnerships and enhance our mutual security. We understand the sensitive nature of the cross-border cooperation, and I want to once again thank all the agencies involved in Guzmán's capture. Now we have an opportunity to further that collaboration and build on the momentum that already exists.

[The statement of Chairman McCaul follows:]

STATEMENT OF CHAIRMAN MICHAEL T. MCCAUL

APRIL 2, 2014

Just last month, the Peña Nieto administration, in coordination with U.S. law enforcement, took down the biggest drug kingpin in the world. "El Chapo" Guzmán was responsible for thousands of deaths, and for violence that stretches across the globe. Leading up to Guzmán's capture, Mexican authorities also arrested a series of his lieutenants. This past July, President Peña Nieto's administration also captured Miguel Angel Treviño Morales, the leader of the Los Zetas cartel. This was the most significant arrest prior to Guzmán's and is indicative of President Peña Nieto's commitment to bringing down the cartels. Now we have an opportunity to examine the bilateral cooperation between our two nations that resulted in this progress, and how we can build upon these successes to further combat the cartels.

I applaud Immigration and Customs Enforcement (ICE) for their participation along with the Drug Enforcement Administration (DEA), U.S. Marshals, the U.S State Department, and Mexican authorities for this capture. The involvement of our agencies stems from the fact that Guzmán's reach went far beyond Mexico's borders. He is Public Enemy No. 1 in Chicago and carries indictments in California, New York, and my home State of Texas.

As we all know, the capture of this drug lord was significant both symbolically and operationally to the Sinaloa Cartel, however we know that drug trafficking organizations like this one will continue on, and are nowhere near extinction. The best way for us to counter them is by working together, and today we are here to examine U.S.-Mexico cooperation in battling the cartels, and the cartel's effects on our homeland security.

Americans understand that the threat posed by drug traffickers is particularly intense along our Southwest Border. These organizations compete against each other for smuggling routes into the United States—creating a war zone that engulfs innocent people living in the region. The spillover violence in the United States stems from a variety of criminal activities which bring people and illicit goods into the country.

Drug trafficking organizations are highly agile. With billions of dollars in capital, these cartels are capable of corrupting officials and responding violently when targeted by law enforcement. Additionally, these organizations are not constrained by boundaries, so often their crimes pass through many jurisdictions—creating an often challenging landscape for law enforcement—and reinforcing the need to work together to counter these criminals.

Cartels like the Sinaloas and the Zetas in Northern Mexico are growing their capabilities and infrastructure and in doing so can facilitate the illicit flow of people, drugs, and weapons across our borders. There is the constant risk of these organizations partnering with Foreign Terrorist Organizations (FTO), and the past arrest of an Iranian national suspected of plotting to assassinate the Saudi Arabian ambassador in the United States allegedly involved Mexican cartel members. This depth and coordination of criminal activity highlights the need for heightened awareness of the narco-terrorist nexus within the Mexican cartels.

Because of the threats to both the United States and Mexico stemming from organized crime, both of our nations share security objectives for our borders—keep threats out, but ensure the expeditious flow of commerce. Our respective law enforcement agencies have been working closely together to come to a common understanding of how to synchronize enforcement operations on each side of the border. However, we cannot just focus on our shared border, Mexico must stop criminals long before they reach us. As Mexico's economy improves, it is now seeing an increase in immigration from Central and South America. This will place a great burden on Mexico to better secure its southern border, and we are working through the

Mérida Initiative to assist in not only technology applications, but operational planning and training to support President Peña Nieto's goals as well as those of the United States.

As we saw last month, the ability to share information between U.S. and Mexico's law enforcement agencies, as well as plan and conduct bilateral operations, is critical to achieving our mutual goal of combating the cartels. As part of that effort, I and other Members of this committee, recently sent a letter to Attorney General Holder and Secretary of State Kerry encouraging them to request Guzmán's extradition to the United States pursuant to the extradition treaty between our two nations. As with several other extraditions of narcotics traffickers from Mexico to the United States in recent years, this cooperation ensures these criminals will never threaten the law-abiding citizens of our two great nations ever again.

With the support of President Peña Nieto, we have the opportunity to work together to continue to strengthen our partnerships and enhance our mutual security. We understand the sensitive nature of the cross-border cooperation, and I want to once again thank all of the agencies involved in Guzmán's capture. Now, we have an opportunity to further that collaboration and build on the momentum that already exists.

Chairman MCCAUL. Without objection, I do want to enter a copy of the letter that was sent to Attorney General Holder and the Secretary of State for insertion into the record.

[The information follows:]

LETTER SUBMITTED BY CHAIRMAN MICHAEL T. MCCAUL

APRIL 1, 2014.

The Honorable JOHN KERRY,
Secretary, U.S. Department of State, 2201 C Street, NW, Washington, DC 20250.
The Honorable ERIC HOLDER,
Attorney General, U.S. Department of Justice, 950 Pennsylvania Ave., NW, Washington, DC 20530.

DEAR SECRETARY KERRY AND ATTORNEY GENERAL HOLDER: We applaud the United States and Mexican administrations on their close cooperation in carrying out the successful operation that resulted in the capture of Sinaloa drug cartel leader Joaquín "El Chapo" Guzmán. The well planned and executed joint operation stands as a tribute to the political will on both sides of the border to tackle organized crime and demonstrates unprecedented coordination between the United States and Mexico. The unrelenting effort to bring Guzmán to justice marks a significant accomplishment in our shared goal of defeating the global illegal drug enterprise that poisons our country and the region.

After thirteen years of eluding capture and directly contributing to devastating violence in Mexico and the United States, it is clear that Guzmán presents an extraordinary threat to the United States and Mexico. Guzmán rightfully deserves to be prosecuted. We understand that your two departments are currently engaged in discussions about whether to seek Guzmán's extradition to the United States. Pursuant to the extradition treaty between the United States and Mexico, we encourage you to formally request that the Mexican Government extradite Guzmán to the United States, where he is facing indictments in multiple states. To date, seven federal districts have brought indictments against him, including the most serious of criminal charges. As you may know, federal prosecutors in New York and Illinois have already publicly said they will seek his extradition.

That Guzmán should be extradited is not unprecedented. In 2007, Osiel Cárdenas Guillen, who for many years headed the storied Gulf Drug Trafficking Organization (DTO) or cartel, was extradited to the United States where he was prosecuted, convicted, and subsequently sentenced to 25 years in prison.

In February 2009, Miguel Caro-Quintero, the reputed leader of the now-defunct Sonora cartel was extradited from Mexico to the United States. He eventually pled guilty to marijuana trafficking and distribution, and is serving a 17-year sentence in a U.S. prison.

In 2010, Mexico extradited Jesús Vicente Zambada-Niebla to the United States. Zambada-Niebla had been arrested in Mexico in March 2009 and is facing charges in the United States for his alleged role as logistics coordinator for the Sinaloa cartel.

Also in 2010, Mexico extradited the former Mayor of Cancún, Mario Ernesto Villanueva-Madrid, to the United States to face charges of conspiring with the Juárez cartel. Villanueva-Madrid was sentenced in June 2013 to nearly 11 years in prison in the United States. It is our understanding that following completion of his sentence in the United States, he will be sent back to Mexico where he faces additional charges that may require him to spend another 22 years in prison.

In April 2011, Mexico extradited Benjamin Arellano-Felix, a leader of the Arellano-Felix DTO, to the United States to face racketeering, money laundering, and narcotics trafficking charges in California. Less than a year later, he received a 25-year prison sentence in April 2012, which he is now serving in U.S. prison.

And more recently, in March 2013, Mexico extradited Cesar Alfredo Meza-Garcia, an alleged leader of a cell of the Tijuana cartel, to the United States to face the charges against him.

These precedents make clear Mexico's willingness to extradite criminals who have broken U.S. laws to face justice in the U.S., and we ask that you request that El Chapo face this same justice in the U.S. for his crimes.

Once again we commend you and our Mexican partners on this extraordinary success against Guzmán, and look forward to continuing to work with you and others in the Mexican Government to bring him to the United States for trial.

Sincerely,

MICHAEL T. MCCAUL,
Chairman.

PETER T. KING,
Chairman, Subcommittee on Counterterrorism and Intelligence.

CANDICE S. MILLER,
Chairman, Subcommittee on Border and Maritime Security.

PATRICK MEEHAN,
Chairman, Subcommittee on Cybersecurity, Infrastructure Protection, and Security Technologies.

JEFF DUNCAN,
Chairman, Subcommittee on Oversight and Management Efficiency.

RICHARD HUDSON,
Chairman, Subcommittee on Transportation Security.

SUSAN W. BROOKS,
Chairman, Subcommittee on Emergency Preparedness, Response, and Communications.

Chairman MCCAUL. Chairman now recognizes the Ranking Member, the gentleman from Mississippi, Mr. Thompson.

Mr. THOMPSON. Thank you, Mr. Chairman, for holding today's hearing.

I also want to thank the witnesses for their testimony.

But first I would like to recognize Mr. Dinkins, who has served us in a capacity for 25 years at the Customs Service who might be looking forward to a rocking chair or whatever you do when you retire, but we want to recognize you for your service. Chairman said you are too young for a rocking chair, but we do thank you for your service.

On the morning of February 22, 2014, drug trafficking boss and leader of the Sinaloa Cartel, Joaquín El Chapo Guzmán, was captured in Mazatlán, Mexico, a resort town of Mexico's Pacific coast. Guzmán was captured from a Mexican—Guzmán, who escaped from a Mexican prison by bribing prison officials, had been on the run since 2001.

At the time of his arrest, Guzmán was considered the most powerful drug trafficker in the world. Guzmán's arrest was a historic, commendable, joint effort between United States authorities—including the Drug Enforcement Administration, and Immigrations Customs Enforcement, Homeland Security Investigation—and Mexican authorities.

Guzmán's arrest represents a significant victory in the Mexican drug war that has killed at least 70,000 people, including children. Ironically, his capture was completed without any gunfire.

After Guzmán's arrest, the question remains on where he will be prosecuted and if he will be extradited to the United States. A successful prosecution of Guzmán in Mexico could show the world that, under President Nieto's leadership, the Mexican government is committed to taking down the cartels. However, Guzmán is responsible for bringing drugs, including marijuana, cocaine, heroin, and methamphetamines into the United States, and there are seven indictments in five different States against him.

While we await the Department of Justice decision whether or not to seek Guzmán extradition, we need to evaluate what Guzmán's arrest means for the United States and its cooperation with Mexico to combat drug trafficking organization and other transnational crimes.

Although the arrest of Guzmán is encouraging, we must understand that the kingpin strategy of taking down top drug trafficking organizational leaders is not likely to address the cartel problem by itself. Instead, fundamental improvements to Mexico's law enforcement and judicial systems, economic reforms, and other systemic changes will be necessary.

The United States has a vested interest in addressing drug trafficking organizations and their illicit activities in the United States and beyond our borders. While cartel-related violence has not occurred here in the way it has in Mexico and our border communities remain quite safe, narcotics trafficking and associated criminal activities, including human trafficking and human smuggling, occurs in communities across the United States.

Partnering with the Mexicans where appropriate to address the cartel can be an effective method of helping to curb cartel-related activities before it crosses our border. The Mérida Initiative has provided a means for U.S. support through equipment, training, and technical expertise to our Mexican partners.

Within DHS, U.S. Customs Enforcement operates several initiatives aimed at working cooperatively with Mexico to combat the cartels, including operating a border enforcement security task force, referenced BEST, and vetted units within Mexico. U.S.-Mexico security cooperation is essential to addressing the cartels that affect both nations.

It is my hope that this committee continues to find effective ways to support cooperation.

With that, Mr. Chairman, I yield back.

[The statement of Ranking Member Thompson follows:]

STATEMENT OF RANKING MEMBER BENNIE G. THOMPSON

APRIL 2, 2014

On the morning of February 22, 2014, drug trafficking boss and leader of the Sinaloa Cartel, Joaquín El Chapo Guzmán was captured in Maztalán, Mexico, a resort town on Mexico's Pacific Coast. Guzmán, who escaped from a Mexican prison by bribing prison officials, had been on the run since 2001.

At the time of his arrest, Guzmán was considered the most powerful drug trafficker in the world. Guzmán's arrest was a historic, commendable joint effort between United States authorities—including the Drug Enforcement Administration and Immigrations and Customs Enforcement's Homeland Security Investigations—and Mexican authorities. Guzmán's arrest represents a significant victory in the Mexican drug war that has killed at least 70,000 people including children. Ironically, his capture was completed without any gunfire.

After Guzmán's arrest, the question remains on where he will be prosecuted and if he will be extradited to the United States. A successful prosecution of Guzmán in Mexico could show the world that under President Nieto's leadership, the Mexican government is committed to taking down the cartels.

However, Guzmán is responsible for bringing drugs—including marijuana, cocaine, heroin, and methamphetamines—into the United States, and there are seven indictments in five different States against him. While we await the Department of Justice's decision whether or not to seek Guzmán's extradition, we need to evaluate what Guzmán's arrest means for the United States and its cooperation with Mexico to combat drug trafficking organizations and other transnational crimes.

Although the arrest of Guzmán is encouraging, we must understand that the "kingpin strategy" of taking down top drug trafficking organization leaders is not likely to address the cartel problem by itself.

Instead, fundamental improvements to Mexico's law enforcement and judicial systems, economic reforms, and other systemic changes will be necessary. The United States has a vested interest in addressing drug trafficking organizations and their illicit activities in the United States and beyond our borders.

While cartel-related violence has not occurred here in the way it has in Mexico and our border communities remain quite safe, narcotics trafficking and associated criminal activity, including human trafficking and human smuggling, occurs in communities across the United States. Partnering with the Mexicans, where appropriate, to address the cartels can be an effective method of helping to curb cartel-related activity before it crosses our border. The Mérida Initiative has provided a means for U.S. support through equipment, training, and technical expertise to our Mexican partners.

Within DHS, U.S. Immigration and Customs Enforcement operates several initiatives aimed at working cooperatively with Mexico to combat the cartels, including operating a Border Enforcement Security Task Force (BEST) and vetted units within Mexico. U.S.-Mexico security cooperation is essential to addressing the cartels that affect both nations. It is my hope that this committee continues to find effective ways to support this cooperation.

Chairman MCCAUL. I thank the Ranking Member.

Other Members of the committee are reminded that opening statements may be submitted for the record.

[The statement of Hon. Jackson Lee follows:]

STATEMENT OF HON. SHEILA JACKSON LEE

Good morning and welcome. I would like to begin by thanking Chairman McCaul and Ranking Member Thompson for agreeing to convene this hearing on, "Taking Down the Cartels: Examining the United States-Mexico Cooperation."

- I thank the witnesses testifying today, James Dinkins, executive associate director, Homeland Security Investigations, U.S. Immigration and Customs Enforcement, Department of Homeland Security.
- Alan Bersin, assistant secretary of international affairs and chief diplomatic officer, Department of Homeland Security (Democratic witness).
- John Feeley, principal deputy assistant secretary of state for western hemisphere affairs, Department of State.
- Chris Wilson, associate, Mexico Institute, Woodrow Wilson International Center for Scholars.

Thank you all for being here and sharing your expertise with us.

In one of the most atrocious acts of violence against an innocent U.S. citizen, Bobby Salcedo was killed execution-style while vacationing in Mexico by a single gunshot to the head after being kidnapped. Mr. Salcedo was kidnapped while at dinner with family and friends in a restaurant and had no apparent connections to the drug or arms trade.

Mr. Salcedo was a pillar of his community in El Monte City, California where he served on the local school board, and also served as the vice principal and football coach of Mountain View High School. Mr. Salcedo also served as a local leader for such organizations as the South El Monte/Gomez Palacio, Durango, Mexico Sister City Organization.

Furthermore, Mr. Salcedo was in the process of earning a doctoral degree in educational leadership at the University of California, Los Angeles, and had previously earned his bachelor's degree in history from California State University, Long Beach, and a master's degree in educational administration from California State University, San Bernardino.

Violence from the drug trade has also created many problems in my home city of Houston, Texas. Houston has one of the highest murder rates among U.S. cities with a population over 1 million. Furthermore, much of this violence likely stems from the fact that Houston is a major hub for drug traffickers, who supply cocaine, marijuana, heroin, and methamphetamine to distributors in other American markets. Many of these issues surrounding violence also stem from the problem of trans-national gangs and organized crime cartels.

There are currently at least seven drug cartel organizations operating between the United States and Mexico. These groups are not only involved in the illicit transportation of drugs but are also involved in the illicit trade of firearms, execution of public officials and these groups have also terrorized entire local populations.

Many of these gangs and cartel organizations also have vast links and networks within the United States, some even managing to penetrate American junior high and high schools. It is important that we recognize this threat and work towards the dissolution of these groups and continue to promote legitimate trans-national trade and exchange.

I would like to commend the Mexican government under the leadership of President Felipe Calderón for having significantly increased their efforts to stop the drug cartels and end the violence, deploying some 45,000 troops and 5,000 police throughout Mexico. We in the United States will continue to support the Mexican government as we did in 2012 when over $1,300,000,000 was appropriated to the Mexican government to fight the illicit drug trade. This money was appropriated under the Mérida Initiative to help break the power of the drug cartels, assist the Mexican government in strengthening its military organizations, to help improve the capacity of its justice system, curtail gang activity in Mexico, and to diminish demand for drugs in the region.

It is important that we continue to work vigilantly towards breaking the illicit drug trade links and networks between the United States and Mexico while working together to create a bright future through legitimate commercial and financial trade between our two great nations. I am quite confident that through a concerted effort towards increasing trans-national trade and creating opportunities in the legitimate sector we can work towards a brighter future for both the United States and Mexico.

The lack of bi-national coordination, in effect, provides cartel leaders a sanctuary south of the border. Without much better coordination with Mexican law enforcement on the most important cases involving the leaders of the cartels, they will continue to make a mockery of our border defenses.

One goal which would be specific enough to give a clear idea of whether we were succeeding or failing would be the arrest, prosecution, and incarceration of Chapo Guzmán, the notorious leader of the Sinaloa cartel. Such a goal, clearly stated and unequivocal, would provide focus and accountability to the efforts and would force a close working relationship among law enforcement across the border. If U.S. forces can find Osama bin Laden, I am sure, with Mexican help, they can find and arrest Chapo. After all, *Forbes* magazine publishes his photograph in its annual edition on the world's billionaires. That arrest would do more to stop the flow of contraband into the United States and the slaughter in Mexico than all the billions spent so far. With Chapo and other cartel leaders in custody awaiting trial, the Obama administration could validly proclaim that it has made the border materially safer.

Time is of the essence. The cartels are gaining significant authority within some areas in Mexico, and the Mexican people understandably tire of the bloodshed and cost of fighting them. I have little doubt that, when the Calderón administration ends in just over a year, Mexico's commitment to the fight against the cartels will wane significantly, if not actually come to an end. In addition, the cartels are rapidly diversifying into new lines of criminal activity, taking over the production and sale of pirated music CDs, videos, and software. They steal and distribute petroleum and hijack commercial trucks on an unprecedented scale. As they diversify, the cartels become harder and harder to isolate from the mainstream economy and harder to close down.

This is the time for a maximum coordinated push. Border defense is far more than just playing a deadly version of Red Rover. One of the consequences of the hysteria about border security is the build-up of the Border Patrol at the expense of Customs enforcement. The emphasis on protecting the long stretches of remote border between the official crossings (or "ports") has a price. With the de-emphasis on Customs inspections at the ports and the resulting strain on Customs and Border Protection (CBP), more contraband gets through the ports.

Always opportunistic, the cartels have seen and seized the opportunity to put more contraband through the ports of entry. Most of the criminal activity has shifted to the border crossings, not the places in between. As not only a Member of Congress representing the 18th Congressional District of Houston, Texas, but also as the Ranking Member of the Border and Maritime Security Subcommittee, I have become particularly concerned by this misallocation of resources. But, the popular demand is for beefing up enforcement, not better inspections. Moreover, low staffing at the ports has damaged legitimate cross-border trade, with imported goods condemned to sit additional hours waiting to be inspected. By appearing tough—making fortification of the border with additional Border Patrol the top priority, while deemphasizing the ports of entry—it is easier for the criminals to come through our front door. Once again, the symbol has trumped reality.

If the United States wants effective border security more effective law enforcement measures must be taken. By attacking money laundering and making bi-national criminal investigation and prosecution of the cartel bosses a priority, the border can be made significantly more secure.

In the process, the mayhem in Mexico and the smuggling of drugs and people into the United States will be reduced. There must be a unified focus. All agencies must get on the same page for the effort to succeed. State and local law enforcement, with the coordinated efforts of all relevant Federal agencies, can win this. Nothing less will.

I look forward to working with my colleagues on both sides of the aisle to confront the challenges that still lie ahead, to face what is hard, and to achieve what is great. Thank you, Mr. Chairman and Ranking Member Thompson. I yield back the balance of my time.

Chairman MCCAUL. We are pleased to have four distinguished witnesses with us here today to discuss this important topic.

First, Mr. James Dinkins, the executive associate director of Homeland Security Investigations for U.S. Immigration and Customs Enforcement. As the director, Mr. Dinkins has direct oversight of ICE's investigative and enforcement initiatives and operations targeting cross-border criminal organizations that exploit America's legitimate travel, trade, financial, and immigration systems for their illicit purposes. Mr. Dinkins held a number of key leadership positions within ICE, including as special agent in charge for HSI Washington, DC.

I must also note, as the Ranking Member did, that Mr. Dinkins will be retiring this month after many years of service to our Nation.

We thank you, sir, for your service and wish you well in your retirement, although you are young enough to have a second career, I personally think.

Next is Mr. John Feeley, serves as the principal deputy assistant secretary for Western Hemisphere Affairs at the U.S. Department of State. Mr. Feeley has responsibility for the daily management of regional policy implementation and the supervision of 50 diplomatic posts in the Americas.

He has also been the department's director for Central American affairs and deputy director for Caribbean affairs. Mr. Feeley's overseas assignments have included Mexico City; Santo Domingo; Dominican Republic; and Bogota, Colombia.

Thank you, sir, for being here.

Mr. Christopher Wilson is an associate at the Mexico Institute of the Woodrow Wilson International Center for Scholars, where he leads the institute's research and programming on regional economic integration and U.S.-Mexico border affairs. He is the author of "Working Together: Economic Ties Between the United States and Mexico." Mr. Wilson has previously done analysis on the nation of Mexico for the U.S. military and as a researcher in American University's Center for North American Studies.

Finally, we have Mr. Alan Bersin, currently serves as an assistant secretary of international affairs and chief diplomatic officer for the Department of Homeland Security, a position he assumed on January 3, 2012. Previously he served as commissioner of U.S. Customs and Border Protection, where he oversaw operations of CPB's 57,000-employees workforce. Mr. Bersin is a former secretary of education for California, and dear to my heart as an AUSA United States attorney for the Southern District of California.

Witnesses' full statements will be included in the record.

Chairman now recognizes Mr. Dinkins for 5 minutes.

STATEMENT OF JAMES A. DINKINS, EXECUTIVE ASSOCIATE DIRECTOR, HOMELAND SECURITY INVESTIGATIONS, U.S. IMMIGRATIONS AND CUSTOMS ENFORCEMENT, U.S. DEPARTMENT OF HOMELAND SECURITY

Mr. DINKINS. Thank you, sir.

Chairman McCaul and Ranking Member Thompson and distinguished Members of the committee, thank you for the opportunity to appear before you today to discuss the close collaboration between ICE Homeland Security Investigations and our partners in Mexico.

Each and every day, HSI special agents in the United States as well as special agents assigned to our many offices in Mexico exchange investigative information and intelligence with our Mexican counterparts. HSI cannot succeed in combating transnational criminal organizations without strong working relationships, and I can assure you we have the best relationships with our Mexican counterparts as we have had. From Mexican customs officials to the federal police, the prosecutors to the military, each one of these agencies have proven to be a key partner with ICE.

The recent successful capture and arrest of the Sinaloa Cartel leader, El Chapo Guzmán, by the Mexican military and law enforcement did not only send a devastating blow to the Sinaloa Cartel, but it also sent a clear message to the world—a message that Mexico is willing and able to tackle the most sophisticated and brutal drug trafficking organizations that exist.

The United States and Mexico share a unique border, immigration challenges, trade, as well as we exchange cultural beliefs. The nearly 2,000 miles of border between Mexico and the United States is one of the most frequently-crossed borders in the world. That combined with the 46 legitimate border crossings, as well as the harsh desert and mountainous terrain present unique challenges to law enforcement and border security.

A result of these challenges, challenges that both Mexico and the United States face—our relationship has continued to grow and mature with our Mexican counterparts.

While the recent arrest of El Chapo made news around the world, there are many other examples of successful collaboration between Mexico and the United States that are less known but are very important. For example, recently HSI Mexico City received information pertaining to the sexual exploitation of several children. Our investigation revealed that the adult suspect resided in Mexico was posing as a teenager, befriending individuals on-line, and enticing them to provide pornographic images of themselves. He later revealed who he was as an adult and started forcing them and extorting them to provide more obscene materials.

HSI Mexico City provided the investigative lead to a special investigative unit within PGR, the Mexican attorney general's office, who quickly responded, located, and arrested the suspect.

Another example that demonstrates Mexico's rapid response to investigative leads and intelligence came last October during the most recent discovery of a sophisticated, subterranean cross-border tunnel located near Otay Mesa port of entry in California. During the course of that investigation, we developed information indicating that the tunnel was being constructed with an entrance in a warehouse south of the border in Mexico and then exiting through a warehouse in the United States.

We provided that information to Mexico, and within moments the Mexican military responded, located the warehouse and the entrance in Mexico. Collectively in the United States HSI was able to seize 11,000 pounds of marijuana, 149 kilos of cocaine, make three arrests, as well as the Mexican military and law enforcement seized an additional 6,000 pounds at the tunnels entrance in Mexico.

In addition to the exchange of investigative information and intelligence, we also frequently conduct joint training with our counterparts in Mexico. Just 2 weeks ago ICE hosted the third Mexican customs officers training course. Twenty-four Mexican customs officers attended the training course, which is modeled after the HSI special agent training course, which is held in the Federal Law Enforcement Training Center in Glynco, Georgia.

In addition, just last month HSI hosted, with our partners at Department of State, a gang training seminar in Mexico City that was attended by over 300 law enforcement officers from countries across Central America.

These are just two examples of the joint training as well as investigative information sharing that demonstrates the partnership with Mexico continues to grow.

In closing, I want to emphasize that no single agency or country can tackle transnational criminal organizations unilaterally. Rather, it requires a multiagency, multinational approach.

With the capture and arrest of El Chapo Guzmán, Mexico has proven that they not only have the resources and capability, but they also demonstrated that they have the will that it takes to tackle the most significant and dangerous leaders of transnational criminal organizations.

I want to thank you again for the opportunity to be here and I will be happy to answer any questions.

[The joint prepared statement of Mr. Dinkins and Mr. Bersin follows:]

JOINT PREPARED STATEMENT OF JAMES A. DINKINS AND ALAN D. BERSIN

APRIL 2, 2014

INTRODUCTION

Good morning Chairman McCaul, Ranking Member Thompson, and distinguished Members of the committee. Thank you for inviting the Department of Homeland Security's (DHS) Office of International Affairs (OIA) and Immigration and Customs Enforcement (ICE) to testify on the future implications for drug trafficking organizations in Mexico and highlight the solid cooperative relationship the United States and Mexico have established.

First and foremost, we salute the government of Mexico for the February 22 capture and arrest of Joaquín "El Chapo" Guzmán Loera, one of the most wanted men in the world. The Sinoloa Cartel contributed to the death and destruction of numerous lives across the globe. The President's Strategy to Combat Transnational Organized Crime identified Mexican drug trafficking organizations, including Sinaloa and other drug cartels, as a significant danger to the United States and other nations—we must continue our successful, bilateral, efforts to defeat these criminal organizations and reduce their power and influence within Mexico.

During his recent trip to Mexico, Secretary Johnson relayed the administration's message directly to his counterparts: He congratulated them on this historic development; he praised the many Mexican efforts that resulted in the arrest; and he observed that this arrest and capture is emblematic of the many successes Mexico has had in the fight against transnational criminal organizations. As is the case with many complex investigations—and as Mexican officials noted—there was indeed U.S. and Mexican collaboration that led to the arrest. For many years now, U.S. and Mexican law enforcement have been working together to identify and arrest criminals. But let us be clear about this point, the arrest and capture of El Chapo was a Mexican operation and a Mexican success. Mexico deserves the credit. Secretary Johnson communicated this to his counterparts, and we would be remiss if we did not re-emphasize that point with you today. We are pleased with the level of cooperation between the government of Mexico and the United States Government and other departments and agencies. The United States and Mexico will certainly continue to work cooperatively to dismantle drug cartels and criminal organizations.

The United States and Mexico share a historically unique relationship of migration, trade, and cultural exchange. The 1,969-mile border between the United States and Mexico is the most frequently-crossed border in the world. Trade between the United States and Mexico continues to grow, totaling more than $1 billion a day, making Mexico the United States' third-largest trading partner.

The United States and Mexico have strong economic ties. We are their largest trading partner and they are our second-largest trading partner. But those facts only scratch the surface of our economic and trading relationship because in reality we make goods together as a product crosses the border multiple times before completion. The majority of DHS programmatic efforts with Mexico are focused on expediting the legitimate flow of goods and people and interdicting and preventing the illicit flows of people, weapons, drugs, and currency, as well as working with Mexico and Guatemala to improve security along Guatemala's northern border. Mexico and the United States have built a solid foundation and now historic levels of cooperation are on display across the spectrum of both countries' governments, and the U.S.-Mexico border is safer, more secure, and more efficient than it has ever been.

In the last 10 years, the United States and Mexico have revolutionized their security and trade relationship, achieving unprecedented levels of cooperation and success. The concerted reshaping of the U.S.-Mexico bilateral relationship, which began in earnest through the Mérida Initiative, was deepened and memorialized by the Twenty-First Century Border Management Declaration in May 2010 and the creation of the U.S.-Mexico High-Level Economic Dialogue in May 2013. These developments have substantially recast the strategic partnership between the United States and Mexico as one based on the assumption of shared responsibility for, and joint management of, common issues. These principles govern our approach to securing and expediting lawful flows of persons and goods across our common border and are embodied in a series of bilateral agreements entered into by the DHS and the Secretaría de Gobernación (Secretariat of Government, or SEGOB) and Secretaría de Hacienda y Crédito Público (Secretariat of Finance and Public Credit, or SHCP).

This transformation has been largely built on a new understanding of borders within the context of flows of goods and people and not just lines in the sand; a new bi-national approach to border management in which our governments jointly address issues that affect both countries' national and economic security; and direct, sustained, bilateral engagement at the most senior levels of government, including robust DHS engagement. Though we continue to refine bilateral plans, programs, and initiatives to this end—and considerable work remains to be done—remarkable progress has been made.

Transnational crime is not the only shared concern which Mexico and the United States have an interest in addressing together. As highlighted by Presidents Obama and Peña Nieto and Canadian Prime Minister Harper at the North American Leaders Summit, our cooperative agenda includes facilitating the secure flow of people and goods across our borders, increasing economic competitiveness, and expanding educational and scientific exchanges. In each of these areas—trade and travel, security, and exchanges—Secretary Johnson expressed the desire of the United States to work with our counterparts throughout the government of Mexico and stated the intent to maintain and deepen the relationship between U.S. agencies and their Mexican counterparts.

It is important to highlight the Declaration of Principles that Secretaries Johnson and Videgaray signed on March 20, which reaffirms the shared commitment of the United States and Mexico to collaborate on security matters and to continue to promote the economic growth and prosperity essential to both of our nations. Effective customs partnership is the linchpin in our nations' efforts to increase security and economic prosperity and nowhere is this more apparent than at our shared border. The Declaration of Principles will take us to the next level of cooperation, moving from a bi-lateral approach to a bi-national approach. It is built on the principles of shared responsibility and joint border management which underlie our engagement. And it recognizes that security and facilitation are mutually reinforcing objectives.

Through this arrangement, DHS and our Mexican counterpart will, among other things:

- Streamline information requirements and manifest processes, something we are already moving toward through President Obama's Executive Order to streamline the export/import process for America's businesses;
- Deepen the integration of our trusted trader programs; and
- Work with each other and the private sector on infrastructure development and improvements at the ports of entry.

EXAMPLES OF SUCCESS

There are other areas in which we are working with Mexican counterparts. We would like to highlight a just a few examples of success. This will not be a comprehensive list, but is reflective of the depth and breadth of the work we do with Mexico:

- In fiscal year 2010, ICE's international partners played a central role in Operation Pacific Rim. Working closely with the Colombian National Police, Mexican authorities, and our partners in Ecuador and Argentina, as well as the Department of Justice's Federal Bureau of Investigation and Drug Enforcement Administration, ICE led an investigation that spanned the globe and effectively disrupted one of the most powerful and sophisticated bulk cash and drug smuggling organizations in the world. This transnational drug trafficking organization was responsible for nearly half of the cocaine smuggled from Colombia into the United States between 2003 and 2009—approximately 912 tons with an estimated street value of $24 billion. As a result of law enforcement cooperation, both domestic and international, this operation, which eventually spanned three continents, resulted in the capture of the top leadership and other high-ranking members of the Pacific Rim Cartel, 10 convictions, 21 indictments and seizures totaling more than $174 million in cash, 3.8 tons of cocaine, and $179 million in property.
- Customs and Border Protection (CBP) is working with Mexico's Federal Police to enhance public safety in the border region through continued augmentation of the Cross Border Coordination Initiative, which began in April 2013. Through the Cross Border Coordination Initiative, a result of the Border Violence Prevention Protocols, the U.S. Border Patrol works with Mexico's Federal Police to conduct coordinated patrols of our shared border. These joint efforts, in cooperation with other relevant law enforcement agencies, focus on the crimes of criminals and organizations connected with the smuggling and/or trafficking of narcotics, weapons, persons, and bulk cash, as well as help to coordinate humanitarian efforts.
- One of the most effective methods for dismantling TCOs is to attack the criminal proceeds that are the lifeblood of their operations. DHS has worked closely with Mexican counterparts through the ICE Homeland Security Investigations (HSI)-led National Bulk Cash Smuggling Center (BCSC), and the National Targeting Center—Investigations Division (NTC–I) created in December 2013 in collaboration with CBP. Since its inception in August 2009, the BCSC has initiated more than 700 investigations, and has played an active role in more than 550 criminal arrests, 360 indictments, and 260 convictions. The increased HSI

presence at the NTC, which includes HSI's Trade Transparency Unit, enhances the joint mission of CBP and HSI to enforce applicable laws, develop critical intelligence, strengthen relationships with domestic and international partners, and provide law enforcement support during National emergencies.

- In April 2013, DHS signed an agreement with the government of Mexico creating the framework for the Interior Repatriation Initiative. This initiative is designed to reduce recidivism and border violence by returning Mexican nationals with a criminal history to the interior of Mexico, where there is a higher likelihood that they will reintegrate themselves back into their communities, rather than continue their association with criminal organizations on the border. DHS is working with Mexico to explore additional options to refine and modernize our binational approach to repatriation. Those conversations are only just beginning but we are optimistic that the outcome of the dialogue will be a better, more effective, and more efficient repatriation and re-integration process.
- And we are working with our Mexican counterparts to leverage science and technology to expedite legitimate commerce and increase supply chain security. Specifically, we are strengthening our trusted trader programs to include recognition of reusable electronic conveyance security devices as instruments of trade. DHS and Mexican counterparts plan to form a task force to demonstrate the technology and to address any policy and regulation requirements for implementation.

CONCLUSION

Strengthening homeland security includes a significant international dimension. To most effectively carry out DHS's core missions—including preventing terrorism, securing our borders, and protecting cyberspace—we must partner with countries around the world. Through international collaboration—including specifically our work with Mexico—we not only enhance our ability to prevent terrorism and transnational crime, but we also leverage the resources of our international partners to more efficiently and cost-effectively secure global trade and travel. The successes in our partnership with Mexico highlight the importance of DHS's international engagement.

Thank you for the opportunity to testify today. We welcome the opportunity to address your questions.

Chairman MCCAUL. Thank you, Mr. Dinkins.

The Chairman now recognizes Mr. Feeley for 5 minutes.

STATEMENT OF JOHN D. FEELEY, PRINCIPAL DEPUTY, BUREAU OF WESTERN HEMISPHERE AFFAIRS, U.S. DEPARTMENT OF STATE

Mr. FEELEY. Mr. Chairman, Ranking Member Thompson, Members of the committee, since we first met when you visited Mexico, Mr. Chairman, I have been grateful for your and this committee's constant interest in and focus on the very important issue of U.S.-Mexico security cooperation. Your personal knowledge of the border and your own previous experience as a prosecutor have made our conversations rich and productive, and they have contributed to my better understanding of the domestic dynamics that affect that cooperation.

As you are aware, Mr. Chairman, it has been my privilege to serve at our embassy in Mexico on two occasions: First in the days and months after 9/11, when we were forced to reexamine how neighbors must confront the horrors of terrorism in democratic societies; and most recently from 2009 to 2012, when we and our Mexican partners truly transformed our relationship—our security and our commercial relationships in the service of the American and Mexican people.

In my current position as the Western Hemisphere Bureau hemispheric security coordinator I have remained focused on the linchpin that is our work in Mexico in protecting the American people from the threat of transnational organized crime.

I must also thank the U.S. Congress, and again, this committee in particular, for its consistent, bipartisan, strong support of the U.S.-Mexico relationship in general and the Mérida Initiative in particular. Mérida is a success story, and the Congress' commitment to Mérida has been a cornerstone of that success.

Begun under the Bush-Calderón administrations and reaffirmed and now strengthened in the Obama-Peña Nieto administrations, the United States and Mexico coordinate and cooperate to ensure our mutual security in ways, quite frankly, unimaginable to me when I reported to Mexico over a decade ago. This commitment to shared security goals that incorporates respect for human rights—it transcends political parties and extends across both governments' interagency communities.

President Obama's visit to Mexico in February for the North American Leaders' Summit and bilateral meetings with President Peña Nieto marked his fifth trip to Mexico as President and it highlights the importance of our relationship with Mexico. While our bilateral agenda includes a wide array of issues—trade and commercial interests, our shared environment, educational exchanges, and efforts to make us a more competitive partnership in a globalized world—security cooperation has always been a central element of the agenda on each of those trips.

I am pleased to report to you, Mr. Chairman, and this committee that it is working.

The recent arrest—without a shot fired—of the world's most famous drug trafficker, co-leader of the Sinaloa Cartel, Joaquín El Chapo Guzmán Loera, represents a milestone in that cooperation. Not an end-state, not a final victory, but a clear indicator that through cooperation that respects Mexico's and our sovereignty and is conducted in a spirit of trust and shared enterprise, no individual or criminal network is immune from the reach of the law.

We congratulate the Mexican people and their government on the capture of El Chapo Guzmán. This was a Mexican operation conducted by Mexican marines and supported by U.S. law enforcement agencies—among them the marshals, DEA, FBI, and my colleagues at HSI. This is how it is supposed to work.

While the Mérida Initiative doesn't fund law enforcement operations, it does build capacity; it does teach agencies how to work in a task force environment; it does help Mexico produce skilled analysts, investigators, prosecutors, cops, and all the other public servants necessary to implement and strengthen the rule of law in Mexico. This, Mr. Chairman, makes us safer here at home.

At the end of the day, Mr. Chairman, U.S.-provided equipment and hardware is not the panacea for Mexico's still-difficult struggle against organized crime and drug traffickers. What is transforming Mexico's rule of law and making its citizens safer is the development of the human capital of its educational, police, justice, penitentiary, and broader governmental institutions.

If I have learned anything in working with the Colombians in the 1990s, the Central Americans and Mexicans over this past decade, it is that cartels, mafias, transnational organized crimes are parasitical organizations. They need society so that they can obscure their illegal activity and sell their illicit goods and services.

They crave weak government institutions they can suborn and intimidate. Most of all, they seek to establish conditions of impunity that allow them to stay in business as they cross borders freely to exploit the weakest links wherever they can find them.

In this, the Mexican cartels are no different than the Colombian criminal bands or the U.S.-based Cosa Nostra or the Japanese yakuza. They are made up of delinquent individuals who become empowered through the accumulation of illicit wealth, the corruption of law enforcement and judicial institutions, and the fear that they sow among ordinary, law-abiding citizens.

But I am convinced that we are stronger—and by "we" I mean the Mexican and American teachers, community activists, substance use disorder counselors, the beat cops, the law enforcement agents, the prosecutors, and the legislators, and all of the others who collaborate in our binational effort to take away the cartels' ill-gotten gains, to take away their markets, to investigate them, arrest them, prosecute them, and, when convicted, to put them behind bars.

No one from the administration is claiming victory or spiking the ball here. But we have a powerful, tested formula to combat the cartels.

We must constantly improve upon that formula through academic and practical study, through operational vigilance and information sharing. But it will always contain as its central core empowered societies, well-trained and incorruptible public servants, and mutual respect and an ironclad commitment to cooperate across borders.

I thank you again for the opportunity to appear this morning and I look forward to our conversation and your questions.

[The prepared statement of Mr. Feeley follows:]

PREPARED STATEMENT OF JOHN D. FEELEY

APRIL 2, 2014

Mr. Chairman, Ranking Member Thompson, and Members of the committee: Since we first met when you visited Mexico, Mr. Chairman, I have been grateful for your and this committee's constant interest in and focus on the very important issue of U.S.-Mexico security cooperation. Your personal knowledge of the border and your own previous experience as a prosecutor have made our conversations rich and productive and have contributed to my better understanding of domestic dynamics that affect that cooperation. As you are aware, Mr. Chairman, it has been my privilege to serve at our embassy in Mexico on two occasions, first in the days and months after 9/11 when we were forced to re-examine how neighbors must confront the horrors of terrorism in democratic societies; and most recently from 2009–12, when we and our Mexican partners truly transformed our security and commercial relationships in service of the American and Mexican peoples. In my current position as the Western Hemisphere Bureau's Hemispheric Citizen Security Coordinator, I have remained focused on the linchpin that is our work with Mexico in protecting the American people from the threat of transnational organized crime.

I must also thank the U.S. Congress, and again, this committee in particular, for its consistent, bipartisan, strong support of the U.S.-Mexico relationship in general, and the Mérida Initiative in particular. Mérida is a success story, and the Congress' commitment to Mérida has been a cornerstone of that success.

Begun under the Bush-Calderón administrations, and reaffirmed and strengthened now in the Obama-Peña Nieto administrations, the United States and Mexico coordinate and cooperate to ensure our mutual security in ways unimaginable when I first reported for duty in Mexico City over a decade ago. This commitment to shared security goals that incorporates respect for human rights transcends political parties and extends across both governments' interagency communities.

President Obama's visit to Mexico in February for the North American Leaders' Summit and bilateral meetings with President Peña Nieto—his fifth trip to Mexico as President—highlights the importance of our relationship with Mexico. While our bilateral agenda covers a wide array of issues—trade and commercial relationships, our shared environment, educational exchanges, and efforts to make us a more competitive partnership in a globalized world—security cooperation has always been a central element of the agenda on each of those trips, and I am pleased to report to you that it is working.

The recent arrest—without a shot fired—of the world's most famous drug trafficker, coleader of the Sinaloa Cartel, Joaquín "El Chapo" Guzmán Loera, represents a milestone in that cooperation. Not an end-state or final victory, but a clear indicator that through cooperation that respects Mexico's sovereignty and is conducted in a spirit of trust and shared enterprise, no individual or criminal network is immune from the reach of the law.

We congratulate the Mexican people and their government on the capture of "El Chapo" Guzmán. This was a Mexican operation, conducted by Mexican Marines, and supported by multiple U.S. law enforcement agencies, among them the Marshals, DEA, HSI, and the FBI. This is how it is supposed to work.

If I have learned anything working with the Colombians in the 1990s, the Central Americans and the Mexicans in the last decade, it is that cartels, mafias, organized criminals are parasitical organizations. They need society so that they can obscure their illegal activity and sell their illicit goods. They crave weak government institutions they can suborn and intimidate. Most of all they seek to establish conditions of impunity that allow them to stay in business, as they cross borders freely to exploit the weakest links wherever they can find them. In this, the Mexican cartels are no different than the Colombian Criminal Bands, or the U.S.-based La Cosa Nostra families, or the Japanese Yakuza. They are made up of delinquent individuals who become empowered through the accumulation of illicit wealth, the corruption of law enforcement and judicial institutions, and the fear they sow among law-abiding citizens.

But I am convinced we are stronger. And by we, I mean the Mexican and American teachers, community activists, substance use disorder counselors, beat cops, law enforcement agents, prosecutors, and all the others who collaborate in our binational effort to take away the cartels' markets, strip them of their ill-gotten gains, investigate, arrest, and prosecute them—and when convicted, put them behind bars.

No one from the administration is claiming victory or spiking the ball here. But we have a powerful tested formula to combat the cartels. We must constantly improve upon that formula through constant study, vigilance, and information sharing. But it will always contain as its central core empowered societies, well-trained and incorruptible public servants, and international respect and commitment to cooperate.

While the Mérida Initiative does not fund law enforcement operations, it does build capacity. It does teach agencies how to work in a task force environment. It does help Mexico produce skilled analysts, investigators, prosecutors, cops and all the other public servants necessary to implement and strengthen the rule of law in Mexico. And this makes us safer here at home, Mr. Chairman.

PEÑA NIETO SECURITY STRATEGY

In August 2013, President Peña Nieto presented the framework of his 10-point security strategy which includes:
- Crime prevention and social reconstruction;
- Effective criminal justice;
- Police professionalization;
- Transformation of the prison system;
- Promotion and coordination of citizen participation;
- International cooperation on security;
- Transparent statistics on crime rates;
- Coordination among government authorities;
- Regionalization to focus efforts; and
- Strengthening of intelligence to better combat crime.

President Peña Nieto's strategy emphasizes coordination and consultation with State and regional governments as key to its security strategy. And we couldn't agree more. As part of the effort to enhance the transition to a more effective adversarial oral justice system, President Peña Nieto promoted the federal legislation to create a uniform criminal procedures code, passed in February 2014. His strategy also focuses on police professionalization by seeking to create a career professional service, consolidating police certification and vetting, elaborating protocols for police action, and creating a national training plan for police.

President Peña Nieto has stated there are no easy solutions or "short cuts" to reduce violence in the short term, instead emphasizing long-term goals such as the rule of law and trust in judicial institutions. In February 2013, President Peña Nieto launched a national multi-tiered crime prevention plan—known as Mexico's National Crime and Violence Prevention Program, led by Roberto Campa—which will include programs to combat poverty, recover public spaces, and increase youth employment. President Peña Nieto has made crime prevention and judicial reform central aspects of his political agenda and has emphasized a focus on reducing kidnapping, homicide, and extortion.

MÉRIDA INITIATIVE

Our security cooperation has been expanding and evolving since the Mérida Initiative was launched in 2008. The Mérida Initiative, above all, a rule of law strategy, in which confronting the cartels is a necessary but not wholly sufficient element of our joint endeavor. It is based on the recognition that our countries share responsibility for combating transnational criminal networks and protecting our citizens from the crime, corruption, and violence they generate. We have based this initiative on mutual respect, and it reflects our understanding of the tremendous benefits derived from this collaboration. We have forged strong partnerships to improve civilian security in affected areas to fight drug trafficking, organized crime, corruption, illicit arms trafficking, money laundering, and demand for drugs on both sides of the border.

The four Mérida pillars that the United States and Mexico agreed to in 2010, and that presidents Obama and Peña Nieto confirmed during President Obama's May 2013 trip to Mexico City, remain our flexible organizing construct:

(1) Disrupting the operational capacity of organized criminal groups;
(2) Institutionalizing reforms to sustain rule of law and respect for human rights;
(3) Creating a 21st Century border; and
(4) Building strong and resilient communities.

Under these pillars, we are accelerating our efforts to support more capable institutions—especially police, justice systems, and civil society organizations; expanding our border focus beyond interdiction of contraband to include facilitation of legitimate trade and travel; and cooperating in building strong communities resistant to the influence of organized crime, with a focus on the youth population.

Our success under the Mérida Initiative is due in large part to the commitment and brave efforts of the Mexican government and the Mexican people to combat transnational criminal organizations. Our Mexican partners have spent at least $10 to every $1 that we have contributed to our Mérida goals in Mexico. That is as it should be; however, the U.S. contribution—none of it in cash and none of it lethal—is vitally important.

Our assistance has provided crucial support to the Mexican government in its efforts to build the capacity of its rule of law institutions and advance justice sector reforms, while enhancing the bilateral relationship and the extent of cooperation between the U.S. and Mexican governments through provisions of equipment, technical assistance, and training. A variety of U.S. Federal agencies—including the Department of State, USAID, the Department of Homeland Security, the Department of Justice, and the Department of Defense—are working with the Mexican government to implement Mérida projects.

By 2011, we began to move away from big-ticket equipment—except for border security—and toward intensive technical assistance and training activities that further Mexican capacity to uphold the rule of law, respect human rights, strengthen institutions, enhance civil society participation, and secure borders. We continue to expand this support to the State and municipal levels in several program areas.

MÉRIDA PROGRAMMING

Under Mérida, we have provided approximately $1.2 billion in equipment, training, and capacity building. At the federal level, Mérida has trained nearly 19,000 federal law enforcement officers, which includes more than 4,400 federal Police investigators deployed throughout Mexico. At the state level, the State Department's Bureau of International Narcotics and Law Enforcement (INL) has supported Accredited State Police Units (PEAs). We have strengthened police academies in the states of Chihuahua, Sonora, Nuevo Leon, and Puebla by providing equipment and training materials, enabling them to serve as the backbone for training programs and to conduct regional training. During 2013, INL provided training to approximately 2,000 state and local law enforcement officers from throughout the country in such topics as officer safety and survival, criminal investigations, crime scene preservations, law enforcement intelligence, anti-gang tactics, anti-drug trafficking, and gender-based violence. INL continues to expand its state-level law enforcement training program, focused on areas such as anti-kidnapping, complementing President Peña Nieto's recently-announced national 10-point anti-kidnapping strategy.

We also continue to build on the success of several on-going programs. For example, Mexico's federal corrections system is now a recognized international leader in corrections reform, with eight federal facilities and six state facilities certified by the independent American Correctional Association (ACA). Mexico has used its success in reforming the corrections systems at the federal level as a launching point for state-level reform—beginning in Chihuahua—primarily by providing basic and advanced correctional training in an effort to achieve ACA accreditation. We will continue to support Mexico in assessing its state facilities and to undertake similar reforms at the state level.

The United States will continue to offer capacity-building support to Mexican security agencies involved in border security, further enhancing their ability to interdict illicit narcotics, arms, and money. We are prepared to support Mexico in their efforts to strengthen the Southern Border, an area the Peña Nieto administration has prioritized, through equipment donation and border management training. We are working with Mexico's Central American partners to implement programs designed to build regional capacity to share information and take action to dismantle transnational gangs, interdict the flow of methamphetamine precursors, investigate international child exploiters, and disrupt cross-border illicit financial flows.

On rule of law, we will focus on supporting Mexico in its transition to an accusatorial justice system by providing robust training to the Attorney General's Office and Mexican law schools, equipping courtrooms with necessary technology for oral trials under the new justice system, and helping to implement the recently-approved federal code. Mexico's ambitious effort to reform its justice system by 2016 requires sustained focus and resources.

The Mexican government strongly advocated for not only the continuation, but the expansion of Mérida's drug court and drug demand reduction programs. Mérida funds have supported the development of Mexican clinical trial networks and funded a comprehensive national survey of inpatient substance use disorder treatment facilities in Mexico and developed a curriculum which has been used to train 600 counselors from six states. The Mexican government is eager to stand up, with the help of the Mérida Initiative, additional drug courts, which use treatment and community support as an alternative to incarceration, throughout the country. Empirical research in the United States and elsewhere has shown that these courts reduce recidivism and save money.

The U.S. Agency for International Development (USAID) has supported the Mexican government in developing and implementing crime and violence prevention strategies in nine communities in target areas in the states of Chihuahua, Nuevo Leon, and Baja California, each significantly affected by drug-related crime and violence. We can take pride in that—while recognizing the far-broader efforts Mexico is itself taking. President Peña Nieto is making this sort of engagement a cornerstone of Mexico's national crime prevention strategy.

USAID has also been working closely with the Secretariat of Interior (SEGOB) on crime prevention and human rights programs. USAID has engaged with Under Secretary for Crime Prevention Campa's team on potential new crime prevention activities that we could support through Mérida, which includes new activities focused on at-risk youth, public opinion polling, and technical assistance on broad crime prevention policy. SEGOB and USAID are discussing a geographical expansion of crime and violence prevention activities, while remaining focused on the testing and replication of such models by the Mexican government and other nongovernmental partners. USAID has also provided direct technical assistance to SEGOB on a human rights assessment that is expected to form the foundation of Mexico's national human rights strategy.

USAID and INL have been working closely with the new Technical Secretary for Criminal Justice Reform Implementation and her team through existing projects focused on institution strengthening, legislative reform, capacity building, civic engagement, and support to law schools and bar associations.

The U.S. Government promotes respect for human rights through our Mérida Initiative and other programming in Mexico. INL trains Mexican state and municipal police officers and state prosecutors on gender-based violence. INL also works to strengthen Internal Affairs units throughout the Mexican government with special emphasis on the police. INL has supported a Department of Justice project to provide training and technical assistance to law enforcement, prosecutors, and judges to combat violence against women and children. The Department of Defense includes modules on human rights in all mobile training events conducted through USNORTHCOM. This training addresses issues such as torture and the appropriate use of lethal force. The Department of Defense also brings Mexican officers to the United States for specialized training on human rights and uses staff Judge Advocates to teach classes in Mexico on human rights and the Law of Armed Conflict. In 2012, USAID launched a Master's certificate program in human rights and security, which was completed by 254 members of the Mexican Federal Police. USAID also began an on-line certificate course on human rights and public security, through which 401 police investigators, from the federal level and the states of Nuevo Leon and Puebla, gained key knowledge and skills on international and national human rights standards, victims' assistance, principles of equality and non-discrimination, prevention of torture, and trafficking in persons.

WAY AHEAD

President Peña Nieto and his team have consistently made clear to us their interest in continuing our close collaboration on security issues and have stated that it intends to give particular emphasis to crime prevention and rule of law. The United States fully supports this further refinement of our joint strategic partnership, and we continue our on-going transition from major equipment purchases toward training and capacity building and an expansion from assistance solely for federal institutions to an increasing emphasis on state and local government. At the same time, the sharing of intelligence and law enforcement cooperation continue apace. The take-down of significant cartel leaders in recent months, most notably the capture of the notorious "Chapo" Guzmán in February, underscores the Mexican government's commitment to confront transnational criminal organizations as it works to reduce criminal violence and enhance citizen security.

In August 2013, the United States and Mexican governments confirmed our shared priorities for Mérida programming. They are: Justice sector reform, efforts against money laundering, police and corrections professionalization at the federal and state level, border security both north and south, and piloting approaches to address root causes of violence.

Since then, the United States and Mexico vetted and approved more than $309 million in 63 new project proposals under the Mérida Initiative. These projects include police training, support for vetting and internal affairs for the police and federal agencies, IT equipment to support oral hearings under the new criminal justice system, forensics, corrections, training for prosecutors and investigators, expanding drug treatment courts, and continued support to Mexico's National Institute of Migration.

Over the past year, Mexico enacted and has begun to implement important anti-money laundering laws which, if enforced aggressively, will give the Mexican government significant new tools to disrupt the operational capacity of organized criminal groups. This offers an opportunity for the United States and Mexico to enhance our partnership by sharing newly available information, and by using this information in a coordinated fashion to further degrade the capabilities of the illicit finance networks of criminal organizations.

The United States and Mexico, working together, have transformed bilateral engagement over the last 10 years, and the Mérida partnership has been an important component of this broader evolution in the relationship. Mexican authorities agree that our cooperation must continue and that the Mérida Initiative provides a comprehensive, flexible framework through which our partnership can move forward to the benefit of both Americans and Mexicans.

Chairman MCCAUL. Thank you, Mr. Feeley.

The Chairman now recognizes Mr. Wilson for 5 minutes.

STATEMENT OF CHRISTOPHER WILSON, ASSOCIATE, MEXICO INSTITUTE, WOODROW WILSON INTERNATIONAL CENTER FOR SCHOLARS

Mr. WILSON. Chairman McCaul, Ranking Member Thompson, Members of the Committee on Homeland Security, thank you for this opportunity to join such a distinguished panel to address the important issue of U.S.-Mexico cooperation to weaken organized crime and strengthen public security.

As Members of this committee know, before dawn on February 22 the Mexican navy arrested Joaquín El Chapo Guzmán, head of the Sinaloa Cartel, which is the most powerful of the Mexico-based transnational organized crime groups. After having escaped from a high-security prison in 2001, Guzmán had taken on a semi-mythical status and many Mexicans believe he was too powerful to ever be captured again.

Because of this, his capture has tremendous symbolic value. The Mexican government has made a powerful statement that no one involved in drug trafficking and organized crime is above the law.

Through the Mérida Initiative, the United States has committed more than $2 billion to support Mexican security forces, criminal justice institutions, border management, and crime prevention. Probably more important, though, than the actual aid package that comprised the Mérida Initiative, was the signal from the two presidents that their military, intelligence, and law enforcement agencies develop stronger relationships.

The Mérida Initiative represented a major shift in the framework for U.S.-Mexico—for the U.S.-Mexico security relationship. Attitudes of mutual recrimination, with the United States faulting Mexico for the northbound flow of drugs and Mexico faulting the United States for the southbound flow of illicit money and arms, gave way to an approach based on shared responsibility for the transnational challenges posed by drug trafficking and organized crime.

In this context, the 2012 election of Mexican President Enrique Peña Nieto, from political party the Institutional Revolutionary Party, or PRI, traditionally aligned with a more limited approach to international engagement, created a degree of uncertainty and apprehension among many U.S. policymakers regarding the future of security cooperation. For some, those fears were stoked by the early move to create a single window for information sharing, meaning that U.S. officials would need to direct communications on security matters through Mexico's Interior Ministry rather than having on-going direct contact with officials throughout Mexico's security apparatus.

Other actions furthered what was a trend toward centralization, a characteristic of the traditional PRI governing style. For example, the Ministry of Public Security, which runs Mexico's federal police, was eliminated as an independent ministry and placed under the control of the Interior Ministry.

Though far from the first sign of on-going engagement with the United States and the new administration, the cooperative binational effort to track down and arrest Joaquín Guzmán is probably the strongest. It represents the culmination of years of effort, but it importantly shows the new mechanisms put in place by the Mexican government to manage intelligence sharing and cooperation at the operational level are functioning sufficiently well to capture Mexico's most wanted criminal.

Day-to-day engagement may be limited, but vitally important cooperation remains strong.

The ability of U.S. and Mexican governments have shown to cooperatively—that the U.S. and Mexican governments have shown to cooperatively generate successes bodes well for the future of bilateral cooperation. Now that things are settling into a new routine on the intelligence-sharing and law enforcement cooperation side, perhaps there is an important opportunity to strengthen engagement on what is known as pillar four of the Mérida Initiative, which is building strong and resilient communities.

To a certain extent this may already be underway. After a long pause in the binational process to create and approve Mérida Initiative projects during the first year of the Mexican administration in 2013, a number of new projects have been agreed upon by the two governments in recent months. Such an approach meshes well with the increased focus from the Mexican government on prevention and the strengthening of civil society, as exemplified by the creation of a new under secretary for crime prevention and citizen participation in Mexico's Interior Ministry.

The Wilson Center recently completed a multi-year research project on the role of civil society and the private sector in addressing public security challenges, launching a book entitled "Building Resilient Communities in Mexico: Civic Responses to Crime and Violence." Our research shows that not only must the United States and Mexican governments work together to strengthen public security, they must also build trust and engage with society so that all parties are working in a coordinated and cooperative way.

The biggest remaining challenges lie at the subnational level, where governance and police capacity remain uneven and in many cases quite weak. States like Baja California, Chihuahua, and Nuevo Leon have seen their rule of law institutions significantly strengthened over the past several years, but states like Tamaulipas, Michoacan, Veracruz, and Guerrero still face major challenges.

The Mérida Initiative remains an important vehicle to identify and support trustworthy partners in subnational government and civil society.

Additionally, U.S. engagement with Mexico across a broad range of topics, especially trade promotion and efforts to strengthen North American economic competitiveness, are a vital part of the broader U.S.-Mexico partnership. The Mexican government understandably does not want security cooperation to dominate the bilateral agenda, so the strength of security cooperation is in part determined by the strength of engagement on other topics. If we boost cooperation on economic issues, that creates space for a greater amount of security cooperation without it overwhelming the agenda.

In conclusion, there is currently strong cooperation between the United States and Mexico on issues of organized crime, drug trafficking, and public security. Nonetheless, there is both a need for and space to further strengthen engagement in the areas of institution building and crime prevention.

Thank you. I would like to thank the committee for the time today.

[The prepared statement of Mr. Wilson follows:]

PREPARED STATEMENT OF CHRISTOPHER WILSON

APRIL 2, 2014

Chairman McCaul, Ranking Member Thompson, Members of the Committee on Homeland Security: Thank you for this opportunity to join such a distinguished panel to address the important issue of U.S.-Mexico cooperation to weaken organized crime and strengthen public security.

THE CAPTURE OF JOAQUÍN GUZMÁN

As the members of this committee know, before dawn on February 22, the Mexican Navy arrested Joaquín "El Chapo" Guzmán, head of the Sinaloa organized crime group, which is the most powerful of the Mexico-based transnational organized crime groups. After having escaped from a high-security prison in 2001, Guzmán had taken on a semi-mythical status, and many Mexicans believed he was too powerful to ever be captured again.

Because of this, his capture has tremendous symbolic value. The Mexican government has made a powerful statement that no one involved in drug trafficking and organized crime is above the law. By creating an expectation that those involved in organized crime will be held responsible for the lives they ruin, this event will hopefully deter youth, in both Mexico and the United States, from considering a life of crime.

THE EVOLUTION OF U.S.-MEXICO SECURITY COOPERATION

In 2007, Mexican President Felipe Calderón met with President George W. Bush in Mérida, Mexico, and agreed to greatly increase U.S.-Mexico cooperation in the hemispheric fight against drug trafficking. Through the ensuing agreement, known as the Mérida Initiative, the United States has committed more than $2 billion to support Mexican security forces, criminal justice institutions, border management, and crime prevention. Probably more important than the actual aid package that comprised the Mérida Initiative, though, was the signal from the two presidents for their military, intelligence, and law enforcement agencies to develop stronger relationships. The Mérida Initiative evolved following the election of President Barack Obama, and the close working relationship between the two governments deepened.

The Mérida Initiative represented a major shift in the framework for the U.S.-Mexico security relationship. Attitudes of mutual recrimination, with the United States faulting Mexico for the northbound flow of drugs and Mexico faulting the United States for the southbound flow of illicit money and arms, gave way to an approach based on shared responsibility for the transnational challenges posed by drug trafficking and organized crime.

In this context, the 2012 election of Mexican President Enrique Peña Nieto, from a political party (Institutional Revolutionary Party, PRI) traditionally aligned with a more limited approach to international engagement, created a degree of uncertainty and apprehension among many U.S. policymakers regarding the future of security cooperation. For some, those fears were stoked by the early move to create a single "window" for information sharing, meaning that U.S. officials would need to direct communications on security matters through Mexico's Interior Ministry rather than having on-going direct contact with officials throughout Mexico's security apparatus. Other actions furthered what was a trend toward centralization, a characteristic of the traditional PRI party governing style. For example, the Ministry of Public Security, which runs Mexico's Federal Police, was eliminated as an independent ministry and placed under the control of the Interior Ministry. In fact, just days before the capture of Guzmán, the *Washington Post* published an article entitled, "Mexico law-enforcement partnership grows more thorny for U.S.," describing the "pause" in cooperation and rewriting of the rules encountered by many U.S. officials as they engaged with Mexico on security cooperation.

Though far from the first sign of on-going engagement with the United States in the new administration, the cooperative binational effort to track down and arrest Joaquín Guzmán is probably the strongest. It represents the culmination of years of effort, but importantly it shows that the new mechanisms put in place by the Mexican government to manage intelligence sharing and cooperation at the operational level are functioning sufficiently well to capture Mexico's most-wanted criminal. Day-to-day engagement may be limited, but vitally important cooperation remains strong.

The ability the U.S. and Mexican governments have shown to cooperatively generate successes bodes well for the future of bilateral cooperation. Now that things are settling into a new routine on the intelligence-sharing and law enforcement cooperation side of cooperation, perhaps there is an opportunity to strengthen engagement on what is known as pillar four of the Mérida Initiative, building strong and resilient communities. To a certain extent this may already be underway. After a long pause in the binational process to create and approve Mérida Initiative projects during the first year of the Mexican administration in 2013, a number of new projects have been agreed upon by the two governments in recent months. Such an approach meshes well with the increased focus from the Mexican government on prevention and the strengthening of civil society, as exemplified by the creation of a new under secretary for crime prevention and citizen participation within the Interior Ministry.

The Wilson Center recently completed a multi-year research project on the role of civil society and the private sector in addressing public security challenges, launching a book, *Building Resilient Communities in Mexico: Civic Responses to Crime and Violence* (Wilson Center and Justice in Mexico Project, 2014). Our research shows that not only must the United States and Mexican governments work together to strengthen public security, they must also build trust and engage with society so that all parties are working in coordinated and cooperative ways. The biggest remaining challenges lie at the subnational level, where governance and police capacity remain uneven and in many cases quite weak. States like Baja California, Chihuahua, and Nuevo León have seen their rule of law institutions significantly strengthened over the past several years, but states like Tamaulipas, Michoacán, Veracruz, and Guerrero still face major challenges. The Mérida Initiative remains an important vehicle to identify and support trustworthy partners in subnational government and civil society.

Additionally, U.S. engagement with Mexico across a broad range of topics, especially trade promotion and efforts to strengthen North American economic competitiveness, are a vital part of the broader U.S.-Mexico partnership. The Mexican government understandably does not want security cooperation to dominate the bilateral agenda, so the strength of security cooperation is in part determined by the strength of engagement on other topics. If we boost cooperation on economic issues, that creates space for a greater amount of security cooperation without it overwhelming the agenda.

Similarly, the more the United States can show it is taking seriously its commitments to address issues of drug consumption, money laundering, and weapons trafficking, the more opportunities will emerge for cooperation in Mexico. To advance within the framework of shared responsibility outlined in the Mérida Initiative, actions must be taken to counter organized crime and drug trafficking in both Mexico and the United States.

LOOKING FORWARD: THE IMPLICATIONS OF GUZMÁN'S ARREST

The most important implication of the capture of Joaquín Guzmán is straightforward. He has already been convicted of drug trafficking in Mexico and has allegedly been directly or indirectly been involved in a large part of the organized crime related violence occurring throughout many states in Mexico. He deserves to be in jail, and putting him there helps consolidate the rule of law and accountability in Mexico.

But however important his capture, it is not the end of anything. Drug trafficking will continue. Indeed, past arrests of high-level drug traffickers have led to no discernable decrease in the flow of drugs into the United States. Violence will continue. The number of homicides in Mexico has declined since its peak in 2011, but the homicide rate is still approximately double what it was 10 years ago, and the rise of citizen vigilante groups in states like Michoacán and Guerrero demonstrate that the Mexican state lacks the capacity to adequately respond to public security challenges in the entirety of its territory.

The capture of Joaquín Guzmán should be celebrated, but there exists the possibility that his arrest fuels greater violence. This could occur as the result of further fragmentation within the Sinaloa organized crime group, which is already comprised of various factions. In the past, internal disputes have led to violent divisions, as was the case when the Beltrán Leyva brothers broke away from the Sinaloa organized crime group. Similarly, there exists the possibility that rival criminal groups could seek to take advantage of the transition in the Sinaloa organization and fight for control of drug trafficking corridors currently under Sinaloa's control.

It is too early to judge the impact of Guzmán's capture on the Sinaloa organized crime group or the dynamic among organized crime groups in Mexico, but we should remain vigilant. To do so, we will need to continue to work closely with Mexican authorities to both counter organized crime and build the foundations of resilient communities throughout Mexico.

In conclusion, there is currently strong cooperation between the United States and Mexico on issues of organized crime, drug trafficking, and public security. Nonetheless, there is both a need for and space to further strengthen engagement in the areas of institution building and crime prevention.

I would like to thank the committee once again for the opportunity to speak with you today.

Chairman MCCAUL. Thank you, Mr. Wilson.

Chairman now recognizes Mr. Bersin for 5 minutes.

STATEMENT OF ALAN D. BERSIN, ASSISTANT SECRETARY OF INTERNATIONAL AFFAIRS AND CHIEF DIPLOMATIC OFFICER, OFFICE OF INTERNATIONAL AFFAIRS, U.S. DEPARTMENT OF HOMELAND SECURITY

Mr. BERSIN. Thank you, Mr. Chairman, Ranking Member Thompson, distinguished Members of the committee. We appreciate very much your holding this hearing to examine the implications for drug trafficking organizations in Mexico, the arrest of Chapo Guzmán, and also to provide an opportunity to highlight the really revolutionary change and solid cooperative relationship between the United States and Mexico.

This committee has been a strong proponent of working with Mexico and understands the pivotal importance of this bilateral relationship. Many of its Members live in border States; several live directly on the border and know the importance of the U.S.-Mexican relationship.

Together with my colleagues, we salute the—and with this committee, we salute the government of Mexico for the capture and apprehension of Chapo Guzmán. Secretary Johnson, who has been to Mexico twice in the first 100 days of his service as the new Secretary of Homeland Security, relayed the same message directly to his counterparts.

He congratulated them on this historic development and observed that this arrest and capture is emblematic of the many successes that Mexico has had in the fight against transnational criminal organizations, many of them most recent, as noted by the Chairman—Lazcano, Trevino, El Chayo. These were all major crime bosses in Mexico who are now either dead or in prison.

As is the case in any complex investigation, and as Mexican officials noted, there indeed was strong U.S.-Mexican collaboration that led to the arrest. That should not be surprising to anyone, given the nature of our nations' close relationship.

But one of the signal results of this was the recognition by U.S. authorities in the praise of Mexican authorities; this was a, as Mr. Feeley indicated, a Mexican victory won by Mexican marines and Mexican law enforcement officials. But I want to assure this committee, as my colleagues have, that the United States and Mexico will continue to work cooperatively and that there is, in fact, additional—and significant additional—work to be done.

The relationship between the United States and Mexico is unique. It is historically unique because of migration, trade, family relationships, and cultural exchange. Trade between the United States and Mexico now amounts to more than $1.3 billion a day, making Mexico our second-largest trading partner and making us Mexico's largest trading partner.

Mexico has a growing economy—indeed, the 13th largest in the world today, $1.16 trillion. Estimated by the OECD, in one generation in 2042 that Mexico will have a larger economy than Germany.

It also is a society characterized by increasing success in terms of housing, health care, and education. The country is emerging as a regional leader in the Western Hemisphere.

In the last 10 years Mexico and the United States have truly revolutionized our security and trade relationship. The transformation has been built on smartly managing the flow of goods and people; a new binational approach to border management, which stresses co-responsibility and shared duty and obligation; and No. 3, direct, sustained bilateral engagement among the highest leaders of both countries. The institution building is underway and will continue.

Transnational crime is not the only shared concern which Mexico and the United States have an interest in addressing together. Significant efforts have focused on expediting the lawful flow of goods and people and interdicting and preventing the illicit flows of people, weapons, drugs, and currency, as well as working with Mexico and Guatemala to improve security along Guatemala's northern border.

DHS continues to have a robust and mutually-beneficial relationship with our counterparts in the government of Mexico based on these new doctrines of co-responsibility and co-migration—the co-management of migration issues and crime issues.

Strengthening homeland security includes a significant international dimension. To most effectively carry out DHS's core missions—keeping dangerous people and dangerous things away from the American people—we must partner with countries around the world. No more important is our relationship with Mexico and developing that relationship as we move forward.

Thank you very much, Mr. Chairman and Ranking Member. I look forward to responding to your inquiries.

Chairman MCCAUL. Thank you, Mr. Bersin. I appreciate your closing comment that no more—relationship is more important than with Mexico. It is just right south of our border. The Middle East, halfway across the world, impacts our homeland security, but Mexico is right there.

Let me just say first to Mr. Dinkins, I want to thank—or congratulate you and your agents for a job well done taking down the largest drug kingpin that we have ever known—one of the biggest threats to the world. Quite frankly, I think it should have gotten more news. It is a big deal and I just want to say, you know, thank you to you and your agents for what you did.

Mr. Feeley, I appreciate your leadership on the Western Hemisphere, working with Roberta Jacobson, and my good friend at the State Department, on this issue. You know, I chair this committee but I also chair the U.S.-Mexico Interparliamentary Group and we meet with the Mexican congress every year to talk about these important issues, and I want to thank you for that.

I do have to ask, though, starting out, I sent a letter, along with the chairs of my subcommittees, to Secretary of State and the Attorney General requesting that they request extradition of El Chapo Guzmán to the United States of America. When I talked to the ambassador from Mexico, Medina Mora, who is a good friend of mine—former attorney general, former director of CISEN—we talked about this issue; he told me that, startling, that the United States has not requested extradition at that point in time and that he was open to that idea.

Is this administration willing to seek extradition? The reason why it is so important is because we know El Chapo Guzmán was in prison in Mexico under very like circumstances and broke out of prison and remained at large and, as Mr. Wilson said, gained great notoriety by doing that. I don't think that is a wise policy to have him in a Mexican prison where we can extradite him to the United States, put him in a supermax prison, and I would feel very confident, given our Federal prosecutors—and I was one of them—could get him life in prison.

Could you answer that question?

Mr. FEELEY. I certainly can, sir, and thank you for that question. Thank you for your letter. The letter was extremely well-informed and you obviously, as I said earlier, as a prosecutor, know these issues exceptionally well.

We have already here, in multiple instances and from multiple distinguished Members, congratulated the Mexican people and their government on the capture of Chapo Guzmán. It was and remains a significant achievement and a major step forward in our shared fight against transnational organized crime.

The decision whether to pursue extradition will definitely be a subject of conversation with the Mexicans. As you yourself know, sir, the wheels of justice often grind slowly. I will say that in my experience working the extradition portfolios in Colombia, in Mexico over a number of years, we are nothing if not relentless, and that is a good thing and that sends absolutely the right signal.

Extradition is an enormously powerful tool that we have, and that is why the Department of Justice, my colleagues there, and the State Department, we spend so much time working on the extradition treaties to make sure precisely that we can make sure that people who commit crimes, even if they don't come to the United States, but where the effect of their crimes is fest in our communities——

Chairman McCAUL. I agree. My time is limited. With all due respect, are we going to seek extradition or not?

Mr. FEELEY. At this point, sir, that is an issue that is under discussion and it is with my colleagues in the Department of Justice. I will tell you that all I can say is look to the past and the way in which we have relentlessly pursued criminals.

Chairman McCAUL. Well, I would strongly encourage both the Secretary of State and the Attorney General to do so.

Mr. FEELEY. Message received.

Chairman McCAUL. Thank you.

Mr. Dinkins, a lot of people think this threat is south of our border, it is not in the United States at all. Can you very briefly tell us about the threat in the United States with not only the Sinaloa but with all drug cartels and MS 13 gangs?

Mr. DINKINS. Yes, sir. I think a lot of times people in the United States look south and they think it is an issue of—that it is a problem in Mexico, but the reality is, is those organizations live and breathe right in the towns—right here in the District of Columbia,

New York, Atlanta. They are in their communities. That is where the drugs are being smuggled into, being distributed by the organizations, and being sold, as well as gangs taking over territory and enforcing the distribution networks for the different cartels.

So this is a U.S. problem as much as it is a Mexico problem. It is also a problem that we need to wean ourselves off of the—look at ourselves and say, "Why is there such a demand for these types of drugs in our communities?"

Chairman MCCAUL. Yes, I agree. I think the fact that Chicago labels him "Public Enemy No. 1" shows that it is in the heartland of the United States, as well.

Mr. Wilson, I thank you for your testimony. There have been speculation, I think early on in the new administration, comparing Peña Nieto to Calderón, that there was some speculation that he was not going to be as tough on the cartels, that he was going to bring down the violence but couldn't explain how or how he could accomplish that. Now, obviously the capture of both the Zeta Cartel leader and El Chapo Guzmán I think maybe changes that narrative.

Can you tell me what the difference in strategy is in cooperation between the Calderón administration and the new administration?

Mr. WILSON. Sure. Thank you for the question.

I believe there is actually a great degree of continuity between the two presidencies and the type of cooperation that exists.

Of course, over time in Mexico, as the Calderón administration confronted the organized crime groups there emerged really a public security crisis because of the number of murders that were associated with the fight that resulted between cartels, between criminal organizations. So the primary challenge that President Peña Nieto confronted entering office was bringing down the levels of violence, of extortion, of kidnappings that were really wreaking great harm on society.

So that has been his goal. The approach, as we have seen, has actually continued to be going for the top-level leaders and mid-level leaders of criminal organizations. At the same time, they have developed a strong program that is really just beginning to bear fruits in terms of crime prevention, creating a new portion of the Interior Ministry designed specifically to look at how they can use programs for social development, job creation, anti-crime programs targeted at youth, et cetera, to really prevent violence in the first place.

So that is something that is still on-going, but it is really important to highlight that there has not been a weakening of the intensity of the effort to root out organized crime under the new administration.

Chairman MCCAUL. That is good to hear. I think the recent captures demonstrate that.

Mr. Feeley, last question: Pablo Esobar probably rivals notoriety with El Chapo Guzmán. He got taken down in Colombia. After that time there became an unraveling within Colombia of the cartels and the Medellín Cartel.

Can you tell us whether this event, the capture of El Chapo Guzmán, that there is any analogy there, or will this just be like the head of the Hydra being cut off and another one grows back?

Mr. FEELEY. Thank you, sir. An excellent observation.

December 3, 1993, I was in Colombia when Pablo Escobar was killed by members of the Colombian army. What we saw in the decade after that has been referred to by social scientists and crime experts as the atomization of cartels.

As you know, sir, cartel really is the wrong name for what we face in Mexico and Colombia today. They don't collude to fix markets or to fix prices. They fight among themselves, quite frankly.

With the take-down of Pablo Escobar, that left in the vacuum Cali Cartel. They were taken down. Extradition was an enormously important aspect of that take-down by the Colombian state with the support from the United States.

As I said earlier, there is a formula to this that we constantly refine. Much of what we do in Mexico we learned from our experience in cooperating with the Colombians.

The issue of the Hydra is one that you do have to look at very seriously. What we learned in Colombia and we practice today is that it is not sufficient to do what used to be called "kingpin strategy" only; you must attack the networks. You have to go after the money. You have to focus on prevention, as well.

In the early years of our cooperation in Colombia we focused on kingpin. We morphed that and developed it as the enemy reacted, as we reacted to their sort of shifting and changing.

I think it is fair to say that if you look at the development of the Mexican cartels—and again, we know it is an erroneous term—but it started out as a cartel, the Guadalajara Cartel, back in the 1990s when they took over the sort-of ownership of the product, the cocaine coming out of the Andes. They went from being just merely subcontracted transportation experts to being the owners, the distributors here in the United States.

One final comment I would make is that it is very difficult to predict, obviously, what will happen. But I will say this: Experience has shown that when you take down a figure like Pablo Escobar, or Chapo Guzmán, or any of the other number—Osiel Cardenas—you find that the guys who come up behind those leaders very frequently aren't as good, meaning that they don't have the organizational skills, they don't have whatever the intimidating or the co-opting power that the leader had.

In short, it is not easy to be a cartel leader, and so as you take them out you have to hit it from the top and you have to hit it from the bottom.

Chairman MCCAUL. In closing, I think the good news story here is that not only did we take out El Chapo Guzmán but a lot of his underlying associates——

Mr. FEELEY. Absolutely correct, sir.

Chairman MCCAUL [continuing]. As well. Thank you, Mr. Feeley.

Chairman now recognizes the Ranking Member.

Mr. THOMPSON. Thank you very much, Mr. Chairman.

Assistant Secretary Bersin, last month the full committee held a hearing on human trafficking. As you know, drug trafficking organizations often engage in other crimes, such as human trafficking and human smuggling.

We had a local sheriff who testified before this committee that said comprehensive immigration reform would help address that problem. How would comprehensive immigration reform affect drug trafficking organizations, in your opinion?

Mr. BERSIN. Mr. Ranking Member Thompson, the connection between the smuggling of people I think is directly connected to the prospects for comprehensive immigration reform. To the extent that there is a legitimate labor market, legitimate and lawful ways to come into the country, you would see a decrease in the amount of smuggling of aliens.

With regard to human trafficking, though, I think we are dealing with a different phenomenon. When people are being trafficked for purposes of labor exploitation or sexual exploitation or any of a variety of other illicit means, that is the kind of organized criminal activity that will take place unless stopped by and countered by law enforcement actions.

So I think in analyzing the effect of immigration reform we should distinguish between the smuggling of people—of illegal migrants and the trafficking in human beings.

Mr. THOMPSON. Well, okay. So if we had a different pathway to citizenship, that would help on the side of the criminal element. Is that your testimony?

Mr. BERSIN. Yes, sir. There is no question that the law enforcement efforts that have been applied in a bipartisan method over the last 20 years have increased the cost of being smuggled into the United States by an extraordinarily high level—perhaps five or six times what it was 20 years ago. So there is a direct connection, yes, sir.

I am pointing out, though, that immigration reform won't solve certain forms of human trafficking and we have to remain vigilant on those.

Mr. THOMPSON. I understand. But it is one of the building blocks to reduce it?

Mr. BERSIN. No question about that, sir.

Mr. THOMPSON. Thank you.

Mr. Dinkins, again, we want to thank you for your service, and I am sure we will see you somewhere in the future.

Can you tell us some of the other ways DHS is working with the Department of Justice and the Mexican government to dismantle the cartels and other organizations like them?

Mr. DINKINS. Absolutely, sir.

First of all, we attack the gangs that are actually supporting protection for the distribution of the narcotics in the United States on our streets. We actually last year we seized $1.3 billion in currency, in monetary instruments; 80 percent of that was linked to narcotics smuggling. So that is a huge amount of money that we are taking right out of the pockets of the cartels.

So as Mr. Feeley stated earlier, you can't just look at the kingpins and the organizations themselves; you have to hit them more at all angles and they are diversified in the criminal activities that they do, and you have to address each one of those different criminal activities.

Mr. THOMPSON. Thank you.

Mr. Bersin, in light of what was just said, does the Mérida Initiative, in your words, go far enough toward dealing with some of these things or do you think there are some other things we could do?

Mr. BERSIN. The Mérida Initiative, as you know, Ranking Member Thompson, was the first security sector assistance program between the United States and Mexico, and it has contributed significantly to the success that we have examined here today. To the extent that we continue those programs and there remains funds in the pipeline for the Mérida Initiative, as Mr. Feeley can describe in greater detail, we need to continue to provide this kind of capacity building, these kinds of equipment and technologies that are assisting the Mexican government.

I think we need to continue. There seems to be sufficient funding for this fiscal year and the next. But we need to maintain this as a long-term institutional relationship between our governments, recognizing, though, sir, that Mexico, with the 13th-largest economy and a $1.16 trillion economy, is increasingly able to take care of its security needs on its own wallet.

Thank you.

Mr. THOMPSON. Thank you.

But you—and I thank Mr. Freeley—you do support this notion of cooperation between governments as something that absolutely has to continue?

Mr. FEELEY. Undeniably so, sir. I would just simply point to Colombia. Our relationship with Colombia, in terms of cooperation and transfer of human capital—skills, leverage, technical assistance, et cetera—has been going on since 2002. The funding for that is on a downward trajectory.

Just as Mr. Bersin said, as these countries stand up their own abilities to deal with their own internal rule-of-law situations, the requirement for U.S. technical assistance, expertise, hardware naturally drops off. But these programs—and there are four in the Western Hemisphere: There is one for Mexico, called Mérida; there is one in Colombia—we now re-baptized it, it used to be called Plan Colombia, it is now called the Colombian High-Level Strategic Security Dialogue; we have one focused on Central America; and we have one focused on the Caribbean.

They are the essential vehicles for us being able to build the partnership relationships that we need with host governments so that they can be our partners in keeping their citizens and the American people safer.

Mr. THOMPSON. Thank you.

I yield back, Mr. Chairman.

Chairman MCCAUL. Thank the Ranking Member.

Dr. Broun is recognized for 5 minutes.

Mr. BROUN. Thank you, Mr. Chairman.

Mr. Feeley, I am going to go back to a question that the Chairman asked you about the extradition of El Chapo.

We all know there is a tremendous amount of money in these drug cartels. I don't think anybody will deny that. I don't think anybody will deny how much influence a tremendous amount of money can have in corrupting individuals within the judicial system, within the military system, within the policy system itself.

Frankly, I think it is absolutely unconscionable that this administration has not already asked for the extradition of El Chapo. I think their not doing so, you all not doing so, ranges from just irresponsibility all the way up to incompetence.

I am not convinced that El Chapo will remain in prison. It is my understanding that when he was in prison before he continued to operate his drug cartel and was just as effective in prison as he was out of prison.

It is absolutely critical, if we are going to have some resolution, if we are going to break down this cartel, if we are going to stop the influence of El Chapo and his cartel and any other cartels, we not only have to get people like him extradited to the United States and put them in a supermax, as the Chairman has suggested, as well as get their underlings also brought to the United States where they can be prosecuted, where we will know that we can chop the head off of this poisonous snake.

Frankly, I am not convinced from what you have told us already that that is going to happen. I hope that—my whole message is that we have got to get this drug kingpin extradited to the United States so that he can be prosecuted and that he can be dealt with because he is a killer, he is one who has not only been involved in outright killing of individuals within the cartel's function, but he is a killer of American citizens in promoting their drug and their alcohol—well, not alcohol, but their drug business here. He is killing children's lives with the sex trafficking and the other things that this animal is doing. We have got to get him here.

Please assure me that we are going to just not talk about it, as we have been doing. As you said, there are discussions. Let's get him here. Ask for the extradition.

I think it is incompetence to not do so. Please tell me that you are going to do this quickly.

Mr. FEELEY. Dr. Broun, I very much appreciate the frustration that you feel, and I understand—I absolutely concur in your description of the evil menace that Chapo Guzmán and others like him represent to the American people.

I would simply offer that at the essence, what you are talking about and what we are talking about is a question of trust and confidence in our partners. I would offer the following reflection. The answer that I have is still the same one, and it is I work for the State Department; extradition is the purview of the Department of Justice but we work collaboratively in it so I am not trying to worm out of this at all.

We will be in discussions with the Mexicans regarding the extradition of El Chapo Guzmán. I assure you of that.

Those discussions may not produce the immediate transfer of him for the following reasons: He has also committed the same atrocities on the Mexican people, and the——

Mr. BROUN. Mr. Feeley, my time is about to expire. I appreciate your——

Mr. FEELEY. Sure.

Mr. BROUN. I am going to have to cut you off because my time is limited. I have 1 minute left.

Mr. FEELEY. I hear you.

Mr. BROUN. The thing is, the operative word that you just gave me was "we will." We should have been already. It is past time, way, way past time.

As soon as he was arrested there we should have begun that process. This is something that is absolutely critical for the security of American citizens not only in the border States, but in my own home State of Georgia.

I am an addictionologist. I treat people that have been affected by this animal.

We have got to get him here and try him and have—go through the due process. But once that due process occurs, let's get him here, and having him sit in Mexican prisons—hopefully you are right, but I don't know. I don't think anybody knows whether it is going to occur because there is so much money involved, so much graft and corruption that can be bought through this cartel.

Get him here. Get him here quickly so that we can try this animal in our courts so that he gets his just due.

Mr. Chairman, I am out of time. I yield back.

Chairman MCCAUL. I thank the gentleman.

Chairman now recognizes the gentlelady from California, Ms. Loretta Sanchez.

Ms. SANCHEZ. Thank you, Mr. Chairman.

Mr. Chairman, I would like to begin by asking unanimous consent to submit for the record a report by the California Attorney General's Office entitled "Gangs Beyond Borders: California and the Fight Against Transnational Organized Crime." It is a thoughtful report about what my home State is doing to combat these criminal enterprises, from anti-money laundering to the role local and State law enforcement has in coordinating with their Mexican counterparts, and I would like—I would ask that the report be set into record.

Chairman MCCAUL. Without objection, so ordered.*

Ms. SANCHEZ. Mr. Secretary, California has been at the forefront of coordination on the State level with Mexican officials regarding these transnational criminal networks, and all—you know, money laundering, false IDs, moving guns, people, et cetera. What coordination does our Department have in engaging with our border States to make sure that they have support as they are trying to deal with some of these MOUs and programs that they themselves are putting in?

Mr. BERSIN. Ms. Sanchez, as you know, there is close cooperation in not only California but also in Texas and Arizona and New Mexico between Federal and State authorities, both in—at the level of the Department of Homeland Security, Homeland Security Investigations, which Mr. Dinkins heads up, Customs and Border Protection, which includes both the field operations and the Border Patrol.

In each of the corridors—in each of the border States, but within each of the zones in each of those States—there are close liaison groups involving the knitting together of State, local, county, and Tribal law enforcement to confront the threats presented by transnational criminal organizations. They coordinate with the so-called high-intensity drug trafficking area groups. But, as you

---

*The information has been retained in committee files and is available at *https://oag.ca.gov/ transnational-organized-crime*.

know in California, there are many other instances in which we see this coalescing of Federal and State efforts.

The information exchange has never been better in terms of State and local law enforcement with Federal authorities, and I trust that will continue, recognizing, as you suggest, how critical it is to the struggle against transnational criminal organizations.

Ms. SANCHEZ. Thank you, Mr. Secretary.

I also have a question going back to something that Chairman Thompson asked about earlier, and this is the whole issue of human trafficking. We know that these transnational criminal networks do a lot more than just drug traffic; they do whatever is profitable. If it is profitable to move guns, they will move guns; if it is profitable to move people, they will move people. It is the same network, pretty much, that they are using to move these people across our border.

A few years back now, maybe 10 or so, there was a big crisis or a big spotlight on El Paso, what is deemed as one of the safest cities in the United States, versus the city of Juárez, which was, of course, one of the most dangerous cities in the world. You know, there were these missing women or these women who had ended up dead or couldn't be found, et cetera.

We continue to see in California and other border States this movement of women who are trafficked a lot for the sex trade. We read reports where there are bars that are very—on our side of the border where women are brought and drugged, and hotel rooms by the 30 minutes, et cetera.

What are we working on to ensure that this—that we are cutting into this really disgusting sex trafficking that happens on a nightly basis from, in particular, women from Mexico who are trafficked over and used, but we also see young women from our own big cities being trafficked down there for the same purpose?

Mr. BERSIN. Ms. Sanchez, you are correct. Some have characterized the human trafficking for sex purposes as the newest and greatest threat that we have seen that has accelerated in its importance over the last 10 years. Indeed, as you suggest, there is a special place in hell for those who engage in the trafficking of human beings for sexual exploitation purposes.

The United States Department of Homeland Security and the Department of Justice, as well as the Department of State, have mounted significant efforts to counter this trend. Recognizing the link, which you also posited, between organized criminal groups that regulate the movement across the plazas from Mexico into the United States to see the connection between those and these trafficking groups has been a special focus, for example, of HSI, Homeland Security Investigation investigators.

The State Department, together with the Department of Homeland Security, have promoted something called the Blue Campaign, which is an international effort to publicize the horror of the crime, the means and methods of the crime, and the need to combat it not only with our officers, which we do—so parenthetically, CBP officers, those at the 320 airports, seaports, and land ports, actually have been specifically trained to keep their eyes peeled for the telltale signs of young women who are being brought into the country for the purposes of sex trafficking. So you have a combination of public service campaigns, public announcements that are being capitalized in Central America and in Southern Mexico, that warn against this.

So the crisis that you suggest, the horror of sex trafficking, is recognized, and while we can always do more, there are significant efforts to counter it underway.

Ms. SANCHEZ. Thank you, Mr. Chairman. I think this is just such a travesty that this operates on our—mostly on our side of the border, with respect to this. I would hope we might be able to find a way in which we can buttress our local law enforcement to really go after these hotel operators, these bar operators that know this is going on and it just never seems to stop.

I want to give not only an indication to Mr. Dinkins about moving on, but also thank you for the work that you guys are doing with respect to those investigations.

Chairman McCAUL. We thank the gentlelady for raising that issue. We had a field hearing in Houston on this issue and it was very powerful, moving, including victims' testimony. I intend for this committee to move legislation on that issue, as well.

Ms. SANCHEZ. Great. I would like to work with you on that.

I have some other questions with respect to other issues. I will submit them for the record.

Thank you, gentlemen. Yield back.

Chairman McCAUL. Thank the gentlelady.

Chairman now recognizes the gentleman from Pennsylvania, Mr. Perry.

Mr. PERRY. Thanks, Mr. Chairman.

Thank you, gentlemen, for your appearance and thanks for your service.

I am going to probably go a little bit off the script just to gauge your knowledge on a particular program that I find interesting in Homeland, which—Mr. Dinkins, are you familiar with the unmanned aerial systems role that the Department uses? Can we talk about that a little bit?

Okay, well I will ask these questions and see—first of all, do you know, do we operate any of the vehicles—I mean, I have seen—and if this is Classified, that is appropriate, let me know. But I have seen some of the tracks that we use to move the vehicles around the country, because they might be—you know, they might be down south and we need them north or vice-versa, what have you.

But I am unclear as to whether we only fly on our side of the border or if there are occasions to fly on the other side of the border, so to speak, outside of United States airspace. Can you speak to that at all?

Mr. DINKINS. Sir, unfortunately I can't. I am a consumer of using those when I need support from CBP, but——

Mr. PERRY. Okay.

Mr. DINKINS [continuing]. They provide the service that I need and I am not sure what operation requirements that they need and have.

Mr. PERRY. Because we work and collaborate with, let's say—if we say Mexico, or Canada, for that matter, and let's say an operation that this El Chapo guy—maybe if he was close to the border, was that something that you would request the use of the drone for, and do you know of any times when it has flown into Mexican or Canadian airspace? Have you ever requested in that regard or have all your requests been on our side the border?

Mr. DINKINS. Ours would be on our side of the border.

Mr. PERRY. Okay.

Mr. Bersin, do you have——

Mr. BERSIN. Yes. I actually can speak to this because the program is under the auspices of Customs and Border Protection, and I had the honor for 2 years of serving as the commissioner.

With respect, sir, I suggest that, given to the full details of the implications of the questions you are asking, that that best be held in a less public setting. The fact is that it is one of the very important programs for situational awareness that the Department of Homeland Security has built and it has served both in natural disaster settings, such as monitoring the floods in the north, as well as for border security purposes in the south.

For further details, in terms of its use in connection with external activities, I would suggest that we do that in a nonpublic setting.

Mr. PERRY. That is fair. I will request that from the Chairman.

Let me ask you this, since you seem to have a little bit of knowledge: I also am concerned about the capability, so to speak, and the cost associated with the aircraft, in particular is the MQ–9B. It has got about a 66-foot wingspan, which is longer, by far, than this—it is about three times as wide as this room is and it carries 4,000 pounds.

Now, generally speaking, I think the payload is a camera, generally speaking, but the winglets hold—or the wings hold—wing stores can hold a significant—about a 4,000-pound payload. Do you know what the—how they determined that was the correct asset to purchase for the mission?

Mr. BERSIN. I do not, sir. I will say that the UAVs that I am familiar with, and the ones I believe that CBP utilizes, are the so-called Predator, but you have—so that the one that you describe is one that, frankly, I am not familiar with.

Mr. PERRY. That is the Predator.

Mr. BERSIN. Okay.

Mr. PERRY. That is a designation for——

Mr. BERSIN. Well, that is the examination of its utility for monitoring purposes, both in the case of natural disasters and for security purposes, I think was the subject of significant review in the first part of the 21st Century, when the decision was made to acquire that asset. But I cannot give you the full technical description of how that was assessed.

Mr. PERRY. Okay.

Mr. Dinkins, anything to add?

Mr. DINKINS. Sir, unfortunately I don't have any——

Mr. PERRY. Mr. Feeley, go ahead.

Mr. FEELEY. Sir, I can add one thing. I agree with my colleagues that for a full description of the operational aspects of this, a less public setting is appropriate.

However, the Mexican government has, on two occasions that I am aware of, recognized that the use of unmanned, unarmed aircraft from the United States have been requested and delivered by

U.S. service providers, including CBP. This was back in I believe it was 2010, 2011, their secretary of interior was brought before their congress. As you are aware, there is always an issue of sovereignty when you deal with Mexico, and the idea that there would be unmanned aircraft flying over Mexican airspace that Mexican officials were not aware of, I can tell you that does not happen.

On the occasions when there is a request for aerial surveillance, it is always strictly coordinated, it is requested by the Mexicans, and we do our best to comply.

Mr. PERRY. I will conclude with this, Mr. Chairman.

So it is your understanding or knowledge that we have flown into Mexican airspace upon request of the government?

Mr. FEELEY. Yes, sir.

Mr. PERRY. Okay. Thank you.

That concludes my question, Mr. Chairman. I yield back.

Chairman McCAUL. Chairman now recognizes the gentlelady from Texas, Ms. Jackson Lee.

Ms. JACKSON LEE. Thank you very much.

Let me thank the Chairman and Ranking Member for a very timely hearing.

Again, to the gentlemen making their presentations, thank you so very much for your presence here.

I will add my appreciation, Mr. Dinkins, for your service. You have certainly been before our committee, but as well, you have served this Nation and served it well. Congratulations to you on your tenure.

This is an area of interest, particularly for those of us from the State of Texas, because we have a conflicting and conflicted relationship with our dear friends in Mexico. We have a vigorous and vibrant interaction on the border with respect to travel, trade, friendship, education, and exchange.

I serve as the Ranking Member on the Border and Maritime Security Subcommittee, but even before that would spend a lot of time from the days of a—as a local elected official traveling back and forth and engaging with local elected officials in Mexico. So it has a ring of being a neighbor, and I think that is an important aspect of what we do here today. But at the same time, we have challenges that I think should be better solved—or could be better solved because we are actually friends.

So I have a series of questions—or allies, as you would. Certainly it has been enhanced when the NAFTA agreement was passed between Mexico, Canada, and the United States. I want to remind all my good friends that Mexico is in North America. So we have a stronger relationship than one might think.

Let me also indicate that I was out of the room just for a moment. Lauryn Williams, a U.S. Olympian, is visiting my office, and so I wish her well and I thank the Members for their courtesies on that.

But let me just go directly to Mr. Feeley and pose a question of— extradition is a harsh word. So I would like to ask it in this term: It is clear that we have the infrastructure to hold Mr. Guzmán. Mr. Guzmán has had an international presence. He has caused the devastation and loss of life on both sides of the border.

We are two nations that are in North America. Wouldn't it be appropriate—not to step on the sovereignty of Mexico; that is not the intent—but to be very firm to say that in working as friends we can, as a friend, with your collaboration and input and necessary infrastructure in place, try Mr. Guzmán that would cover the devastating acts that he has—and deadly acts—has perpetrated in Mexico here in the United States? In fact, I would almost insist that we make that proposal to the present president and find a way not to negotiate up but to negotiate in a lateral way, saying, "How do we get this done?"

So, Mr. Feeley, where are you with that? Because when I listen to your testimony are were suggesting it is on the table, it is down the road. I frankly believe it should be on the table and done. Please help me understand why we have not moved more swiftly on that issue.

Mr. FEELEY. Absolutely, Ms. Jackson Lee, and it is a pleasure—it was a pleasure to welcome you in Mexico when you came and we went up to Los Pinos in the last administration, and I thank you for your continue interest in Mexico.

Let me begin by a—perhaps offering a point of comparison. In 2002 Osiel Cardena Guillen, the founder and the boss of the Gulf Cartel, another very powerful——

Ms. JACKSON LEE. Mr. Feeley, I have a short period of time. I need you to jump quickly——

Mr. FEELEY. Got it. I am going to go fast. He was arrested in 2002; he was extradited to the United States in 2007.

Ms. JACKSON LEE. All right.

Mr. FEELEY. The Mexicans have got Barbie, they have got—which is a nickname for a very well-known drug trafficker. The Mexicans, through Mérida, have improved their penitentiary system significantly since Chapo Guzmán escaped from Puente Grande in Jalisco state a number of years ago in 2001.

We have significant trust and confidence that the Mexicans are able to hold him, and we also do respect that the descriptions that Dr. Broun and yourself have made of the damage and the horror that he and his drug trafficking cartel have visited upon the American people—he has also done that to the Mexican people. So it is in full respect, as partners, that we will discuss his possible extradition in the future.

We are allowing, again, as partners, the Mexicans to hold him.

Ms. JACKSON LEE. Thank you.

Mr. FEELEY. We will do everything to help them do that.

Ms. JACKSON LEE. Let me get my last question in—last effort of questions.

But let me say to you the Mérida has worked well. Let me again emphasize that I believe we should move more swiftly toward extradition here to the United States with all respect for the sovereignty and friendship of our friends.

But let me just ask this question about the intermingling of human trafficking, sex trafficking, and what I call modern-day slavery that becomes part of the business now of cartels, which means that now our children—both Mexican children and women—many of you may have remembered or do remember our colleague, Hilda Solis, who gathered us as women on the enormous killings of Mexican women alongside of the border. We have never solved many of those problems or many of those cases, and those cases were under the jurisdiction of Mexico.

Now you have a cartel that, even with Guzmán—so my question is this: Is the cartel still alive? I would ask those who want to—Mr. Dinkins or Mr. Bersin or any of—cartel still alive? How much fear—and we had a hearing on this; I want to again thank the Chairman on this hearing—how much fear do we have that now this business will be expanded into sex trafficking, human trafficking, smuggling, and slavery?

If someone can answer that, I would—No. 1, is the cartel still alive? Guzmán is gone, or at least arrested.

Then this other business that is growing.

Mr. FEELEY. Very quickly, ma'am, the cartel is still alive. Of the major trafficking groups, this is the cartel that most exclusively focuses on drug trafficking as opposed to expanding into other areas, such as sex trafficking. The ones most associated with that tend to be the Zetas, who operate in and fight for territory all throughout Mexico.

You are absolutely right that they are intertwined, and that is why the overall investigative rule-of-law capacity building has to continue to be able to address everything that is moved along illegal networks.

Ms. JACKSON LEE. Mr. Dinkins, any comment?

Mr. DINKINS. Yes, they are still alive but they are on the run.

Ms. JACKSON LEE. The human smugglings? Are you seeing that?

Mr. DINKINS. You know, the great thing about combating the human smuggling, as you know, and I applaud your passion behind it because that is what it is taken, is the awareness that has been brought to the attention, so we are able to nip it at a lot of—at the bud really quick so it becomes not profitable for any organization because there is no ability to actually traffic the victims to begin with.

State laws, Federal efforts, Blue Campaign awareness—you know, our arrests are up 400 percent in 4 years for human trafficking, and it is because of the combination of all that coming together.

Ms. JACKSON LEE. I thank you.

Thank you, Mr. Chairman. I yield back.

Chairman MCCAUL. Gentlelady.

The gentleman from South Carolina, Mr. Duncan, is recognized.

Mr. DUNCAN. [Off mike.] All right. We will start that over.

Iran and Hezbollah have penetrated countries in Latin America and the Caribbean region, and they are exploiting the loose border security measures and cooperating closely with drug cartels and other criminal networks in the region. In February the commander of the U.S. Southern Command testified before Congress and he said this: "Hezbollah has long considered the region a potential attack venue against Israeli and other Western targets," but he admitted U.S. intelligence gaps in truly knowing the full awareness of Iranian and terrorist support networks in the region.

So the question I have for you, Mr. Feeley, is, with so many reports of connections between Mexican drug trafficking organizations and Islamic terrorist groups, namely Hezbollah, what impact do you see El Chapo's capture having on Iran or Hezbollah's activity and ability to exploit the leadership vacuum to further their influence in the region with the drug cartels and other criminal networks? I will point directly to the assassination attempt of the Saudi ambassador here in this country coming through the Southern Border using the Mexican drug cartels.

So if you could speak to that?

Mr. FEELEY. I certainly can, and I thank you for the question. It is an extremely important one.

I thank you for your leadership in keeping focused on the threat of Iran's influence in the Western Hemisphere.

In point of fact, sir, after a number of years service in Mexico I have come away from that convinced that it remains an enormously important task for the entire interagency to stay focused on this. But what we have not seen is the deep development of an Iranian network, whether cellular or centralized, in Mexico that is cooperating with the cartels.

The case to which you referred, Manssor Arbabsiar, which is now an open case—the charging documents are up on the internet; he is now serving a very long sentence in the United States. What that indicated was that he was, in fact, a lone agent. Now, that does not make him any less dangerous and nobody is saying that because he was caught that that is it, game over.

We must use all of the resources we have of the intelligence community, the FBI, HSI, DEA, because that nexus is always there and it will always be there and we need to look at it.

But again, when he came through he thought he was dealing with Zetas. In fact, he was not. There is no evidence to indicate that he ever made contact with them; he in fact made contact with a DEA undercover agent.

So again, I appreciate your focus on this. We remain seized of this issue and our Mexican counterparts, who, I must say, in that—I was in the embassy and I helped direct part of that operation. Our Mexican counterparts—that was a watershed for us—they stood up—they have absolutely no desire to make Mexico or to allow Mexico to become any kind of hotbed of Islamic extremism that can come across the border, hurt us, hurt the Saudi ambassador here at Cafe Milano, as was his stated intent.

So they have worked with us extremely well, and that was the first watershed case, and the result of it, much like the result of the Chapo Guzmán operation, my observation is it only bound us closer together.

Mr. DUNCAN. Well, I appreciate that. The Mexican authorities told Chairman McCaul and I that same thing when we were visiting with them a year or so ago.

I want to reference California's attorney general report that Ms. Sanchez put in the record, and it is highlighting the growing operation of Mexican drug cartels with street gangs. So have you seen Iran or Hezbollah seeking to exploit this growing relationship through mosques or cultural centers in the United States?

Mr. FEELEY. I would defer to my law enforcement colleagues for the U.S. perspective.

In Mexico, no we have not. There are a number of small gangs that operate; they are not at the level of the cartels—Barrio Azteca, Mesicles. They operate up along the border.

They tend to be transnational in that they do cross. Many of them are American citizens and they live and work on both sides of the border, as does much of that community, as Mr. Chairman knows.

We have not seen any indication that they are being penetrated or even approached by the cultural centers. In Mexico——

Mr. DUNCAN. In the essence of time, let's let Mr. Dinkins answer, as well. Thank you for that, Mr. Feeley.

Mr. DINKINS. No. We have not seen that in the United States. I think a driving factor behind that is, it is not in the interest of any drug trafficking organization or any type of criminal enterprise to introduce somebody that is going to do harm to the consumer, and ultimately—so it is—while they are probably not beyond it, it is not in their interest to do so and so we have not seen that type of association.

Mr. DUNCAN. Thank you guys for that.

In the essence of time, last question: The new leadership—how do you see that playing out? You mentioned that you didn't think it had the skills necessary for organization and other things, but from a law enforcement standpoint, how do you see the new leadership of the cartel?

Mr. DINKINS. You know, I think as we take off their leadership, and as Mr.—as we have heard today, is that it takes a special skill set to build an organization, and it is a lot less to actually have folks that are just simply within the organization that are going to step up. We need to make it to—heading an organization is like when you read on the back of cigarettes, it is bad for your health. Same thing as heading up a drug trafficking organization in Mexico, and they are making that.

So they are going to get less-qualified people; it is going to cripple them long-term. As you—law enforcement persists to attack them at every angle they will eventually crumble and resort to— you know, we can't stop crime, but they will resort to the bloodshed that they have been accustomed to.

Mr. DUNCAN. So you don't think El Chapo had a successor that he was training and grooming for an ultimate leadership position?

Mr. DINKINS. I am sure that there are people willing to step up into that vacuum, but they are going to be less qualified and less effective.

Mr. DUNCAN. We will see how that happens.

Mr. Feeley.

Mr. FEELEY. Sir, I would just add, there are indeed some folks that are out there: Ismael Zambada; Esparragoza, known as El Azul. These are folks who have been around for a long time. The Federation, or the Sinaloa Cartel, is perhaps the most developed and most organized of all of the cartels, and, as I said earlier, it sticks very closely to what it does best, and that is moving drugs.

It is not the most shockingly violent; it is not the one that gets involved in human trafficking. It is depraved and it will use violence and intimidation when it has to.

The folks who are currently—we believe, we assess—currently running the show have been around for a while. It is not like it is their first rodeo. But they are under multiple indictments and we are going after them, with our Mexican counterparts, as hammer and tongs, as we went after Chapo.

Mr. DUNCAN. Okay. Thank you.

I yield back.

Chairman MCCAUL. I thank the gentleman.

Let me just, if I could comment on, Mr. Dinkins, the ads on the carton of cigarettes. If people in the United States knew that when they purchased cocaine and other narcotics in the United States that they were actually complicit with violence and the horrific killings of individuals in a very grotesque manner, I would advocate that sort of advertisement campaign. I haven't seen it to date and it is something I am actually very interested in.

With that, the Chairman now recognizes the gentleman from Louisiana, Mr. Richmond.

Mr. RICHMOND. Thank you, Mr. Chairman. Thank you for calling this meeting.

I will just pick up where Congressman Duncan left off. The void that is there—do you all anticipate any increased violence, either from other cartels moving in or within the ranks of El Chapo's cartel, in terms of a power battle to fill that void?

Mr. FEELEY. Our DEA colleagues aren't at this table right now. They obviously have got a very primary role in doing this, and some of the very best analysis that I have seen as a State Department consumer comes from DEA as well as from HSI, FBI, and the whole of Government.

My understanding of the current scenario is that there probably isn't going to be a really nasty knock-down, drag-out fight for leadership simply because there were a couple of these individuals that I mentioned who are long-time confederates of Chapo Guzmán.

He also has several sons who have been involved in the business, and much to a traditional mafia or cartel or organized crime model, they tend to keep things pretty close in. Again, because Sinaloa has historically been among the more, if you will, disciplined cartels, I don't think we are going to see a tremendous amount of internecine fighting with the Federation.

What I do think you probably will see—and this has been going on for a long time—is intra-cartel fighting. So there is a good chance that they will see the Sinaloa cartel as a winged bird appropriately weakened, minus their leadership, and other groups may go after them to try and take over the all-important trafficking plazas.

Mr. RICHMOND. That was my question, so thank you for that answer.

Mr. Chairman, for part of my questions—and I think that DEA would be an appropriate entity, because after—and then, Mr. Dinkins, you can comment on it—much as we talk about the cartels and the violence associated with the cartels, we also have to look at, in our own backyard, the war on drugs that has been a dismal and absolute failure, in my opinion, over the last decade.

So we talk about the cartels and the trafficking that comes over. I see in my neighborhood the end-user and the street-level dealer, but the middle man, once it comes over, what—are you all involved at all in that aspect of it?

Mr. DINKINS. Not in the distribution—the domestic distribution; that is DEA's wheelhouse as well as our State and local law enforcement partners.

But I will say, when you look at the war on drugs and we talk about that is we often forget that law enforcement can't solve a social issue, and I think it is—we have been turning to law enforcement, been trying to do education, but at the end of the day we look at law enforcement and we beat ourselves up about what more can we do.

I think a lot of that comes back down to there needs to be examination of what is causing the children to start using the narcotics and drugs in the first place, and we can't arrest our way out of this one.

Mr. RICHMOND. Or incarcerate our way out of this one, which depletes funds that could go to you all and make sure.

The other thing that we have noticed is that you all have identified hotspots on the border, in terms of the major areas where trafficking comes, and I am sure that the cartels adapt and change their routes. How do we adapt and anticipate those route changes and respond to it?

Mr. DINKINS. Yes. We have seen that. We have seen that, for example, on pangas, which are these open-bow vessels that can hold thousands of pounds that used to once upon a time just go from Mexico right into San Diego. We see those vessels going all the way out, carrying thousands of pounds of drugs all the way up the— then just south of San Francisco and the San Francisco area.

So we have adapted, and we shift resources there with our partners at CBP, working with DEA on different intelligence. But we have been able to shift, and the beautiful thing about technology is that it is—it assists the transaction of criminal organizations, but it is also a tool for us to use against them, and we are able to use technology to aid us in that, as well.

Mr. RICHMOND. Mr. Bersin—and this will be my final question— it would be almost similar to my prior one, concerning spill-over violence in our border communities in the United States from cartels. What are our concerns there and what are we doing to address it?

Mr. BERSIN. So briefly, Congressman, there are two types of spill-over violence, one that would involve having Mexican organized criminals come over into the United States and actually shoot up the town. With an exception of quite a while ago now, we have not seen that kind of spill-over violence.

But to the extent that you refer to what you have, which is the effects of Mexican drug trafficking organizations in our communities, in our neighborhoods, there is considerable violence that is generated by the drug distribution activities and the human trafficking activities. To that extent, the local law enforcement, together with Federal law enforcement, is charged with dealing with that species of spillover violence.

So, it is not a norm, then, for the cartels to either have direct involvement or to order violence in our communities. I guess——

Mr. BERSIN. That is correct, Congressman. In fact, the crime records on the U.S.-Mexican border, measured by FBI statistics, are the lowest that they have been. As Mr. O'Rourke will tell you, El Paso and San Diego are among the two of the 10 safest cities in the United States. So we don't see—we have had occasions where we have Mexican criminals coming over and committing crimes, but the mass violence that we have occasionally seen—or frequently seen in Mexico has not occurred in the United States.

Mr. RICHMOND. Thank you.

Thank you, Mr. Chairman. I yield back.

Chairman MCCAUL. Chairman recognizes the gentleman from Pennsylvania, Mr. Barletta.

Mr. BARLETTA. Thank you, Mr. Chairman, for this very important hearing.

Mr. Bersin, let me just say that I disagree that the immigration reform that is being discussed here in Congress will have significant effect on the war on drugs. I say that because I know for a fact that many of these characters, these actors will use fraudulent documentations to hide their true identity.

Don't you agree that if we don't do proper background checks on these individuals, if we are talking about immigration reform, we will never know the true identity of the person, we won't know the history of their country of origin, what they are dealing with. If we are just looking at paperwork, that is not a proper background check, and this immigration reform will never achieve what many are saying it will.

Mr. BERSIN. Mr. Barletta, with due respect, what my comment went to is the interaction between the proposed or potential immigration reform and human smuggling activities, not the impact on drug smuggling.

You are exactly right. When people are cleared for legal status, if that comes to pass, that is going to be a critical element in the mix in terms of just filtering out, so to speak, those who have criminal records. That—without going further, that has been a subject that, as you know, has been discussed and will continue to——

Mr. BARLETTA. That is a deal-breaker for me. I can't go any further with this discussion until they can satisfy me that we are going to do those proper background checks. I don't want to give a legal status to a drug dealer, a gang banger, a terrorist.

You know, how do you separate salt from sugar if you are just looking at papers? We are giving the American people this false sense of security that somehow if we bring people out of the shadows everything is fine and dandy and all these problems are going to go away when, in fact, we are giving them a ticket to use what they are going to do legally, now, in our country.

So I am very careful that—I don't know how we are going to do it on 11 million people. Nobody has been able to tell me that.

Mr. BERSIN. Again, with due respect, I don't think anybody believes that those who have committed serious criminal offenses should be given a legal status——

Mr. BARLETTA. How will we know? How will we know if we——

Mr. BERSIN. Well, I can tell you from my position now in Homeland Security, in terms of the vetting of the million people who cross our borders every day, we have hugely improved methods of determining who presents a high risk. We have federated computer searches that permit us to check all of the criminal records of people. So I think perhaps we should examine those means and methods.

Mr. BARLETTA. None of that has been discussed in immigration reform that I am hearing here on the Hill. You know, it sounds good, "Well, we are going to do background checks on everyone and then we are going to proceed," but nobody has been able to talk about how we are going to do those background checks.

Are we going to go to the country of origin? How are we going to know, if we are just looking at paperwork? It is not going to happen and we are going to let bad people into our country legally.

So I just want to make sure that we have that discussion as we move forward with these talks.

If I can just go on, Mr. Dinkins, I—back in 2005 when I was mayor I had a lot of problems with drug trafficking, gang bangers, you name it. I came down to Washington in December 2005, met with Department of Justice, brought on a lot of these experts in to talk to me. It was great. Spent the whole day here.

At the end of the day I got this nice coffee mug, I got a lapel pin, and was sent home and realized that, you know, it was great to be able to come here but there—at—this was 2005, there was a real disconnect between local and the Federal Government. Now, we are talking about Guzmán and, you know, what he is doing, but let's face it, you know, eventually those drugs get to the local dealer, they go into the streets, they are ruining the lives of children, and they are sucking out the quality of life of communities who cannot deal with the problem.

How can we begin—or maybe you could reassure me that we are—reaching out to the local law enforcement who are really the people, the boots are on the ground, who deal with this and the cost goes to the local taxpayers. It is great that we took this guy out, but I don't feel any better today because I know as long as long as there is that need for the drugs there is going to be some punk selling drugs in our neighborhoods.

If I could just, then, also say, maybe we could use some of this seized money to get people off the drugs, to get them off—you know, let's get the customers not to be customers anymore. If you can talk about that?

Mr. DINKINS. Yes, sir. I agree.

I can tell you that we are working with our State and local partners very, very closely. So I have about over 1,000 State and local law enforcement officers that we actually have cross-designated and trained to have our same investigative authorities to help empower them as well as, I think, proof of that is we have over about 200,000 open criminal investigations at HSI right now; over 60 percent of those come from leads from our partners—from State, local, and other partners. So it is hand-in-hand.

The police on the streets of our communities are the front lines of our defense. They are the ones that I am calling when I have somebody break into my house, the one that I am calling when my daughter is on drugs.

So we have to work closely with them, and we do it in gains, document bills, you name it. In all of our case categories that we are investigating at the Federal level they are our key, key partner, as well as human trafficking.

Mr. BARLETTA. Good. Thank you.

Thank you, Mr. Chairman.

Chairman McCAUL. I thank the gentleman.

Chairman recognizes the gentleman from Arizona, Mr. Barber.

Mr. BARBER. Thank you, Mr. Chairman, and thank you for convening this hearing. I think this is one of the most important topics that we have discussed since I came here in June 2012.

It is a constant issue for me, as one of nine members of the House that has a border district with Mexico, and I remain concerned, as I have said many times in this committee and in hearings, that we still have a huge hole in our border security efforts, and that hole is right in the middle of my district. You could geographically post it at Douglas, east of the New Mexico border—wide-open land, very rugged, very difficult to patrol. I understand that. Two mountains coming out of Mexico that bring the cartels and their drugs right through the ranches that—where the people I represent live and work and other businesses, as well.

So we have to do better there, and I guess one way that I think we can do better—and this is a question, Mr. Dinkins, for you—is that we have a very close working relationship with the people who live and work the land. They have been doing it for generations. They know those canyons, those mountains, that land better than anybody.

This morning I had a conference call—one of my regular conference calls with the ranchers and others stakeholders in the region and the area, and I rely a lot on their feedback about what is really going on, and we have the—obviously we have DHS representatives on the call, as well. But there are slightly different perspectives on what is really happening.

So I guess, Mr. Dinkins, my question for you is: To what extent has ICE engaged stakeholders on and around the border? Do you know if you can comment on what the Mexican authorities have done on their side of the border?

These people know the border. What have we done to make sure their eyes and ears are giving us the information that we can use effectively?

Mr. DINKINS. Thank you, sir. Yes, we are working really collectively with both law enforcement in that region as well as—I know that Secretary Johnson was just down in that area and met with the ranchers associations and so forth.

So we have been actively engaged in getting the information from the subject-matter experts, which are the boots on the ground. We also have a unique skill set there that we use, the Shadow Wolves, to actually—to help track and look for smugglers crossing the border through the mountainous terrains and desert.

So we are actively engaged in that area and I think that we have made a lot of progress in probably the last 5 or 6 years at taking that information from the citizens that reside in those areas and trying to put that into action.

Mr. BARBER. There are two groups—stakeholder groups that were established quite a while ago that meet on a regular basis every month at Douglas and Naco. We also have them in other areas, but those two in particular are relevant to the discussion.

It primarily convenes stakeholders with Border Patrol supervisors and others, and I would hope that ICE might from time to time join that discussion. I think there would be a lot of information gained that would be very useful.

I guess I want to, Mr. Dinkins, continue with you with another question having to do with the emerging and on-going threats that we see from the cartels. In your opinion, what is the latest and most dangerous threat that the United States law enforcement officials face from the cartels and what are we doing to thwart it?

I know that they are very nimble, they have more money than just about anyone, they are very fast at moving into new areas of threat. So could you give us your opinion on what the most dangerous emerging threat is and what we are doing to combat it?

Mr. DINKINS. Yes, sir. I would say that their most major concern remains what it always has been as the bread and butter of their criminal organizations, which is drug trafficking, because it impacts the citizens of our communities and our children.

We remain steadfast at attacking that issue, but we have also seen, then, as we have put pressure and it becomes less lucrative for them that—for them to move into other areas from smuggling, because it controlled geographical areas, so there is human smuggling involvement, as well as we have even seen them in intellectual property crimes, where, you know, the penalty and scrutiny may not be as high but yet the profits remain high.

So we remain steadfast. I think that as we continue to exchange information with our Mexican counterparts and also even beyond, because those issues also come across the southern border of Mexico as well, and we have to take a whole-region approach to combating it and working with law enforcement across the board. Example: Mexico City training, when we had a gang training operation with our Mexican counterparts, we invited law enforcement from the entire region because it is a joint problem.

Mr. BARBER. Thank you.

Mr. Chairman, I yield back.

Chairman MCCAUL. Chairman now recognizes the gentleman from New Jersey, Mr. Payne.

Mr. PAYNE. Thank you, Mr. Chairman.

I would just like to start out—Mr. Feeley, and I appreciate the point you are attempting to make in reference to the extradition of El Chapo. The crimes that he has committed in Mexico—ultimately we have to be considerate that, you know, they have had issues with him in their own country prior to sending him to us, but we want to continue to make the effort for extradition.

But I appreciate what you are saying. The crimes that he has committed in Mexico are heinous, and they have to deal with him in their country as well, so just wanted to make that point.

Mr. Bersin, you know, the Calderón administration made unprecedented commitments to combating the drug trafficking cartels, and, you know, deploying thousands of resources in man hours to thwart that effort, and has worked with the United States very cooperatively. Now, there was a feeling that—a concern that when Nieto came in, the administration, there might be a step back, but it appears that he is as committed as the Calderón administration was.

So how do you categorize the cooperation with the two administrations, comparing the two?

Mr. BERSIN. Thank you, Mr. Payne. I think, as my colleagues have suggested and—the cooperation is at a high level with both administrations. Differences in tone, differences in message, differences in personalities have not detracted from the fact that the relationship between the two governments, both in the trade context and in the security context, is—remains unprecedented.

So I think that when we see the results of the security efforts of President Peña Nieto that have brought down three or four major drug trafficking figures since he has been in office it is a confirmation of the conclusion that you expressed and I concur with.

Mr. PAYNE. Thank you.

Mr. Dinkins, good luck to you as you move forward. You have served this country well and—as a Government employee, and so now I guess you will go out and be a capitalist and make a lot of money.

Let me ask you, you know, we have seen over the years the efforts that our law enforcement have made on the other side of the border, and, you know, much has been made of the security situation in Mexico for U.S. law enforcement—you know, the tragic death of ICE Agent Jaime Zapata and the shooting of ICE Agent Victor Avila.

What is the current security situation in Mexico for ICE personnel, and have additional security measures been put in place to ensure their safety? Because we know this is dangerous business and, you know, the commitment that our ICE agents and other law enforcement agents have made—the commitment to this Nation to help rid that scourge, my concern is their safety as well, as they do this.

Mr. DINKINS. Sir, and I share that concern and that is definitely something that is in the forefront of my mind, and probably the lowest moment in my career was explaining to Jaime Zapata's family in their living room hours afterwards about how he was killed.

With that said is I am somewhat of an open book on this, but I don't want to be an open book in front of the world. So I would be happy to sit down with you personally and give you my perspective on that. I will say that I am comfortable with the situation, or else I wouldn't be sitting here today. But I don't want to expose what we do and what we don't do to anybody.

Mr. PAYNE. Understandable.

Chairman, I will yield back.

Chairman MCCAUL. Thank you, Mr. Payne.

Chairman now recognizes my colleague from Texas, Mr. O'Rourke.

Mr. O'ROURKE. Thank you, Mr. Chairman, for holding this hearing and convening these experts. I wanted to start by following up on a comment made by my colleague and hopefully help disabuse him and anyone else who might hold the notion that we can somehow conflate immigrants and aspiring citizens with criminality, drug dealers, and gang bangers.

You know, as Mr. Bersin pointed out, El Paso is the safest city today; it has been for the last 4 years. That is, I think, in large part because of the large immigrant population we have in our community, not in spite of that.

These immigrants in El Paso and——

Chairman MCCAUL. Will the gentleman yield?

Mr. O'ROURKE. Yes.

Chairman MCCAUL. I don't recall making a comment on——

Mr. O'ROURKE. It was Mr. Barletta——

Chairman MCCAUL. So you are referring your comments to the gentleman from Pennsylvania?

Mr. O'ROURKE. Yes. Yes.

Chairman MCCAUL. Just for the record, I want to make that clear.

Mr. O'ROURKE. Great. I know that as as a fellow Texan you understand that immigrants are part of the strength of our State, part of the reason that El Paso is so safe. These folks are trying to get ahead, make a better life for themselves, create better opportunities for their children, and I think hold a lot of promise and opportunity for us as a country. So I wanted to make sure that I could say that.

I want to thank Mr. Dinkins and the government of Mexico and everyone involved in the capture of Chapo Guzmán. You know, as someone from El Paso who saw what happened to Ciudad Juárez, where more than 10,000 people were killed in the most brutal, horrific fashion imaginable, we have a very strong interest in him being brought to justice. While I think something close to 1 percent of those murders were ever fully investigated or prosecuted, I think it is generally held that he and the Sinaloan organization had a lot to do with the violence in Juárez and the murders that took place.

But apart from bringing him to justice, apart from the symbolic value that Mr. Wilson talked about, the engagement and the fruits of that that we are beginning to see with this arrest, I really want to know what, if anything, is going to change.

Just by way of context—and my colleague, Mr. Richmond, talked about this earlier—you know, we have had a 40-year war on drugs; we had Crockett and Tubbs battling the, you know, cartels and drugs coming in from the Caribbean; we mentioned Pablo Escobar in Colombia—I think we spent $8 billion on Plan Colombia, and they were cultivating and shipping more cocaine at the end of that than at the beginning of the $8 billion.

We suppressed that to some degree, moved it to Mexico. We have captured Chapo Guzmán, and good, for all the reasons that we have stated. What is going to change, in all reality?

I would love to begin with Mr. Feeley and then hear from Mr. Wilson and Mr. Bersin.

Mr. FEELEY. Thank you very much, Mr. O'Rourke. Those are excellent comments.

I will tell you that what I hope changes is a continuation and an acceleration of the trends that we have seen over the last 40, 50 years. First of all, I would like to say we tend to fall into being prisoners of our own language. "War on drugs" is not a term that the U.S. Government has used or espoused for a number of years.

Our policy with regards to drug trafficking and narcotics—transnational narcotics organizations in the Western Hemisphere is one that is guided by an understanding that you don't commit—you don't conduct war on anybody; what you do is law enforcement-based that contains—that includes prevention, education, and the—all of the full spectrum.

Mr. O'ROURKE. Right.

Mr. FEELEY. So if you look at what we have done in this country—and Mr. Richmond was talking about it earlier—cocaine use is down significantly in the last 30 years in this country. But yes, you are right, it continues to come in.

My colleague said we are never going to stop all the crime, but what we can do is get it to where it does not become the exaggerated public security threat. I think as a result of our four mutually supportive regional partnership agreements with our Latin American——

Mr. O'ROURKE. What do you measure——

Mr. FEELEY [continuing]. Slow it down.

Mr. O'ROURKE. This is what I want to get to.

Mr. FEELEY. Sure.

Mr. O'ROURKE. We are spending—and you correct me, I thought it was $1.9 billion, it is $2.1 billion with Mexico on Plan Mérida.

Mr. FEELEY. Right.

Mr. O'ROURKE. We have sent them Black Hawk helicopters, you know, kind of law enforcement material. We are now focused on this last pillar, which I think is far more productive: Improving civil society, their system of justice, their system of rule of law.

All those things are great, and I think that is—especially that last part is a smart investment in Mexico. But from what we measure coming into this United States—you said this capture makes the United States safer. How are you measuring that? Because of his capture are fewer drugs getting in? Because of Plan Mérida are fewer drugs coming into this country?

What are we really doing to address the reasons behind why we began to spend this money in the first place? That is what I would ultimately like to see: How are we measuring—you know, across the board in this country, how are we measuring these vast sums that we are committing to border security, $18 billion; to Mexico, $2.1 billion?

What do I, as a taxpayer, get out of it at the end of the day? I don't know that we have a measurable answer to that. Because of a limit on time I would love to quickly hear from Mr. Wilson and Mr. Bersin on this, as well.

Mr. WILSON. I would just agree that I share the concern that, you know, capturing a high-level criminal drug trafficker does not automatically lead to any reduction in the amount of drugs flowing across the border into the United States. I think that beyond just the symbolic value of the capture, it contributes to the building of the rule of law and the institutions that maintain the rule of law in Mexico, and I think that as a major partner of the United States, as one of the largest trading partners of the United States, as a neighbor, as a country that we share deep social ties with, there is a tremendous value in having a stronger neighbor, and in that way I think we get the biggest value out of the arrest of Chapo, out of the investments in Mexico's institutions and civil society.

Mr. O'ROURKE. Great.

Mr. BERSIN. Congressman, I think the best approach to responding to your very serious question is to look at it in terms of time frame. Just picking up on Mr. Wilson, look what has happened in Mexico in the last generation in terms of it becoming a 51 percent middle-class country, not the impoverished Mexico that we grew up with and thought about.

It has become a democracy. Since 2000 it has a robust, functioning democracy, something that was unheard of a generation ago.

The economy, the economic growth and its importance to us and to the prosperity of North America is something that has taken root in the last generation, such that it will have a larger economy than Germany if the trends continue over the next generation.

So I think the answer is—you ask a reasonable question and the reasonable response is to say that we must manage this satisfactorily, we must have a deterrent that puts law and the rule of law on the front of our approach to these problems, recognizing that it takes a much longer term to deal with the social—underlying social issues that caused the problems, as Mr. Dinkins suggested in response to an earlier question.

Mr. O'ROURKE. Thank you.

Thank you for your responses and your testimony.

Mr. Chairman, I yield back.

Chairman MCCAUL. Chairman recognizes the gentleman from Texas, Mr. Vela.

Mr. VELA. Thank you, Mr. Chairman.

Mr. Dinkins, I have to begin by putting in a plug for one of your agents who is working as a fellow this year in my office. Today he is the keynote speaker at the border sheriffs conference on South Padre Island, and I want to thank you for sharing him with us and with our folks down in South Texas.

Mr. Bersin, I don't want you to take this as a challenge to your testimony because it is one of those incidents that you may just not be aware of, but it is also one of those things we can't keep—turn a blind eye to. But today in Mexico City Javier Garza Medrano is in custody. We have talked a lot about Chapo Guzmán and his arrest.

We had only one murder in the city of Brownsville this year, and although the killing took place in the city of Brownsville, it was masterminded by the cartel bosses in Matamoros, Mexico. It is something we need to keep an eye on because it just happened they came across—seven members of the cartel came across, killed an innocent man because they got the wrong guy, fled back.

But on that note, you should know that on behalf of the Cameron County district attorney, he would like to thank all of our Federal agencies and our counterparts in Mexico who have taken part in that arrest. But I certainly think it is something that we should watch out for.

Mr. Feeley, I wrote a letter to the President before his visit to Mexico in February and yesterday the State Department and Homeland Security responded. In their letter they say that the Mexican government is making significant progress in addressing crime and violence in border cities in the United States.

My question is, they are not referring to the state of Tamaulipas, right?

Mr. FEELEY. Sir, we share your concerns about the violence in Tamaulipas, and we have engaged with Mexican authorities at the highest levels to encourage the government of Mexico to take measures to focus specifically on Tamaulipas. That is right on the border of your district and we are well aware of it.

We have dedicated a significant amount of Mérida programming to Tamaulipas to attempt to try and get them to be able to be more capable in dealing with them. Couple of examples: As you are well aware, the Bureau of International Narcotics and Law Enforcement has provided training to officers from Tamaulipas; they have all gone through the national police training programs. There are more Tamaulipas officers who are attending the national police training program's 2-week police tactics class in Pueblo that we ran just last year.

We have provided, under Mérida, a significant amount of assistance—about $330,000 in equipment—to their police academy in Ciudad Victoria. All of this indicates that we are focused on Tamaulipas.

That said, I am not going to tell you that Tamaulipas is a place where it is safe for Americans to go. Our travel warning that was reissued in January of this year indicates that—January 8, 2014—indicates that we advise U.S. citizens to defer nonessential travel to the state of Tamaulipas.

The progress that we are seeing is slow. It is incremental. It is in building that capacity of state and local police officials and prosecutors and agents and judges in that very difficult state.

Mr. VELA. Well, I am glad you mentioned the travel warning because I think that is something the public needs to know about in terms of being able to assess whether things are getting better there or not, and that way we can start working on what we are going to do about the situation, because the travel warning further says that all United States Government employees are prohibited from personal travel on Tamaulipas highways outside of Matamoros, Reynosa, and Nuevo Laredo due to the tenuous security situation.

In Matamoros, United States Government employees are subject to further movement restrictions between midnight and 6 a.m. United States Government employees—I probably shouldn't read this one, but—may not frequent casinos and adult entertainment establishments.

Mr. FEELEY. It is on the web, sir. You can read it.

Mr. VELA. I know the casinos well, but for fear that my wife may see this someday, I don't know the adult entertainment establishments.

Mr. FEELEY. Duly noted.

Mr. VELA. But, you know, we are limited on——

Chairman MCCAUL. Without objection, so ordered.

Mr. VELA. We are limited on time here, but the travels—there is nothing different today about the travel warning that was issued in January. I mean, it is a pretty serious and critical condition that we need to get the Mexican government to pay attention to.

Mr. FEELEY. I couldn't agree with you more, sir.

Mr. VELA. You know, the mayor of Matamoros, Leticia Salazar, I was just with her not but, you know, a week and a half ago; I was with her economic development administrator night before last. Of course, they had a serious incident in Matamoros just in December where there was a State Department emergency warning about it. I point-blank asked her, "What kind of support are you getting from the federal government in Mexico City, you know, to help deal with the violence and the critical situation you have got in Matamoros?"

The answer was, "None." You know, it is certainly something that I hope we can work—you know, work together on, because I know Mexico is a big country that had great successes. We have had great successes together in Ciudad Juárez, in Tijuana.

You know, but unfortunately, there are other places that it has only gotten worse, and I think—I would like to partner with our Federal Government and with the people in Mexico to do something about it so that we can make those things safe for the people that live there, so that we can make those places safe for those of us who grew up on the border to come back and forth the way we used to.

Mr. FEELEY. I couldn't agree more, sir.

Mr. VELA. I yield.

Chairman MCCAUL. Let me say thank you to the Members.

I want to thank the witnesses.

Mr. Dinkins, I also wanted to give a shout-out to details in my office: Mike Hatfield, Howard Bolick, and Dave Scott, who I understand may be moving back to my home State in Corpus Christi.

I also want to thank Department of Homeland Security, HSI, ICE for their efforts in this historic takedown, and all Federal law enforcement. You are to be commended. This is, again, a very historic event in the war against the drug cartels.

I also know that the government of Mexico and their officials are watching this hearing and I want to take the opportunity to thank them for their cooperation and encourage this new administration to continue its efforts, as we took down the leader of the Los Zetas—or they did. They also took down El Chapo Guzmán, who has been on the most wanted list for decades.

This is historic and the Mexican people and Mexican administration are to be commended for their efforts in this.

I also would end by encouraging them to work with us on extradition. I think it would be very important to do to get him under incarceration where he can never get out of prison and will face justice and a maximum sentence.

So with that, thank all of you for being here today. The hearing will be held open for 10 days; you may have questions in writing to respond to.

Without objection, this hearing is now adjourned.

[Whereupon, at 12:16 p.m., the committee was adjourned.]

APPENDIX

QUESTIONS FROM HON. LORETTA SANCHEZ FOR JAMES A. DINKINS

Question 1. Mr. Dinkins ICE agents, along with other U.S. law enforcement agencies are currently embedded in Mexico, working alongside their Mexican counterparts. What have been some of the challenges agents have encountered when dealing with their counterparts?

Answer. Our relationship with our Mexican government partners—including Mexico's military, local, state, and federal law enforcement agencies—is very robust and positive, particularly at the operational level. While there have been changes in the way in which we engage the government of Mexico (GOM), our agents have fostered a favorable working relationship with their counterparts.

Under the administration of President Enrique Peña Nieto, Mexican federal law enforcement agencies experienced some structural and policy changes as the government of Mexico took a close and deliberate look at the U.S.-Mexico bilateral relationship, including security cooperation and its joint efforts with individual U.S. Government agencies. As part of this review, the Peña Nieto administration instituted a new ventanilla unica ("single window") policy for assistance coordination, which requires all U.S. Government agencies to work through the Ministry of the Interior as a government-wide single point of contact to approve bi-national programs.

Upon taking office, the Peña Nieto administration decided to disband the Public Security Ministry and consolidated a significant portion of the Mexican federal police under the Ministry of the Interior. This impacted some operational-level coordination.

Question 2. Do you feel that Mexican law enforcement officials have the same standard and training on civil liberties and civil rights as our ICE agents do?

Answer. Through the Mérida Initiative, U.S. Immigration and Customs Enforcement (ICE), with the support of the Department of State conducts capacity-building activities with our partners in the government of Mexico, which, in part enable them to establish their own training practices. Since 2010, through the Mexican Customs Investigator Training program, ICE's Homeland Security Investigations International Operations and the ICE Academy have provided such instruction for several classes of Mexican customs officers. This comprehensive training curriculum, modeled after our own training curriculum for our special agents, consists of a rigorous 10-week basic course that covers investigative techniques, firearms training, physical fitness, and practical field exercises.

The purpose of this course is to prepare Mexican customs officers to assume expanded duties and more comprehensive investigative responsibilities. While the curriculum does not solely focus on civil rights and civil liberties, it does cover proper protocols for conducting interviews and field activity. ICE anticipates continuing to assist Mexican customs in standing up their own investigator training course. As ICE does not have specific insight into the training that any of our counterparts may receive from their own country with regards to the legal observances of human rights standards and knowing that each country has differing constitutional requirements and justice systems, we will refrain on commenting on whether Mexican law enforcement officials have the same standard and training on civil liberties as ICE agents.

QUESTIONS FROM HON. LORETTA SANCHEZ FOR JOHN D. FEELEY

Question 1. In legislation I introduced last fall, H.R. 2872, Border Enforcement, Security, and Technology Act of 2013, I included a provision that would ensure that DHS and the State Department work with Mexico to overcome one of their biggest challenges, securing their southern border. One of the biggest challenges for Mexico in combatting cartels is securing its southern border from traffickers and criminals. What steps has Mexico taken to address its southern border?

Question 2. What more remains to be done?

Question 3. What can the United States do to assist this effort?

Answer. Mexico's engagement with Central America on security and migration issues has increased significantly in recent years. Mexico is working with its Central American partners to combat organized crime, including Mexican drug trafficking organizations that have a presence in Central America.

President Peña Nieto has expressed interest in cooperating with the United States and other regional partners to support the Central American countries' efforts to improve security and expand their economies.

Mexico has also been an active participant with the United States in fostering the Central American Integration System (SICA) Regional Security Strategy. The April 2013 SICA—North America Security Dialogue brought together representatives from all the Central American countries, the United States, Mexico, and Canada. The new forum allowed participants to synchronize our efforts and enhanced regional coordination on security programming.

Mexico's southern border strategy is designed to increase Mexico's inspection and interdiction capacities, and reduce drug and human trafficking along its southern border, which currently has 11 formal crossings and more than 370 informal crossings. Mexico's effort to improve security along its southern border includes the construction of 12 permanent naval bases along its southern river borders and the development of multiple choke points in the southern border region to counter illegal migration and drug trafficking.

To date, Mérida Initiative funds have provided $6.6 million of non-intrusive inspection equipment to Mexican officials stationed at the southern border and approximately $3.5 million in mobile kiosks that capture the biometric and biographic data of migrants living, working, and transiting southern Mexico. In addition, the Mexican National Migration Institute is strengthening immigration verification and control operations across points of entry and internal checkpoints, including at the southern border.

Future Mérida Initiative assistance will support Mexico's efforts to increase its interdiction and criminal detection capabilities along its southern border by providing a more mobile, integrated border management system, involving sophisticated non-intrusive inspection equipment and communication technologies, that will allow these agencies to successfully detect illegal persons and goods.

○